The Truth About War

THE TRUTH ABOUT WAR

J. T. Ford

BROADMAN PRESS
Nashville, Tennessee

DEC 13 '71

Dewey Decimal Classification Number: 261.8
Library of Congress Catalog Card Number: 73–95411
Printed in the United States of America
2.JY70KSP

To Mary Helen

without whose encouragement

this project

would have been neither attempted

nor completed

CONTENTS

Citizenship and Soldiery

As a child I pretended to be a soldier. I suppose all little boys do. With a wooden weapon and careless abandon, I joined forces with the other boys in the neighborhood. We engaged in mock battle.

With admiration and near adulation, we studied Washington, Lee, and Grant. We reveled in the courage of Nathan Hale and Sergeant York. We saw freedom secured by combat. Our heroes emerged from the Boston massacre, the Battle of Atlanta, from San Juan Hill and the trenches and foxholes of Europe.

I came to understand that the American saga which began at Concord has been painfully and expensively sustained. It has taken a tortuous route, twisting and curving over mountain and stream. It has been hacked out of the jungle by hand, costly in money, but more so in blood. It has left its heel and hoofprints in the dust, its tire and track marks in the mud.

Moving in convoys down that rutted road of freedom, our soldiers carry on. The sight of them stirs a mixture of pride and remorse in our hearts. We take great pride in their courageous accomplishments—but we are beginning to resent that they have to march at all!

I remember that cold, grey morning when I drove with my firstborn to join their serried ranks. Upon arrival, he retrieved the little bag from the trunk, and I switched to the driver's seat. He stood by for a few seconds—reflecting a mischievous twinkle

9

of doubt. Could his old dad really manage that precious MG Roadster—and safely deliver it to the dealer for resale?

That afternoon, standing in a small room with an American flag in the corner, he raised his right hand and was sworn into the United States Air Force. Our son was now a soldier! We suddenly had a personal stake in the cold war which had suddenly gotten mighty hot.

It wasn't easy for us to send our son to war. Oh, he made it fine! He was a strong, sturdy boy and had the makings of a good soldier. And his letters indicated normal progress in the helicopter training program. In his fifth month, while I was on a tour of the Iron Curtain countries, a cable reached me in Warsaw reporting his selection as airman of the month on a base of twenty-two thousand men! He went straight through—completing his tour without a scratch.

Now he is home, and our second son is in. You might say that the subject is one in which the author's family *is* personally involved!

G. I. Joe

"Greetings," wrote the President of the United States. "You are hereby ordered for induction into the Army of the United States." Millions of young men have received such a letter through the years.

How does it feel to be drafted these days? What is the typical response of young American males? Are they different from their predecessors? What really are they saying? And what are their basic attitudes?

The Vietnam war isn't as popular with the general public as some past wars have been. And after all, inductees are part of the public. Some of them express doubts about the issues at stake in Southeast Asia. Others are convinced that our cause is just and our procedures are proper. Most of those who don't have an opinion simply reflect their confidence in "our leaders."

"If the President says it has to be done, that's enough for me," is a typical response from a small town southerner. Or, "If you gotta go, you gotta go."

A study of a cross-section sampling of inductees turned up some interesting and encouraging information. Apparently being drafted today feels about the same as it did during World War II when about ten million men went through the experience. The pattern has scarcely changed.

Some of the fellows found induction to be frightening; most found it inconvenient. It was hard to leave family, friends, and familiar surroundings. Some were just getting established in a trade or a vocational training program.

But most of the men spoke freely of their duty to serve their country in such a significant role. They reflected a sense of pride in qualifying physically, mentally, and morally.

Some were excited by the prospect of travel and adventure. Some expressed hope that they could better themselves through military educational and training opportunities. The general impression upon scanning the profiles of this representative group of men was a healthy balance between realism and resignation.

The officers at induction stations and the recruiters who daily enlist men in the respective branches reflect almost unanimous praise for today's American soldiers.

"They're the finest I've seen," commented one processing officer. "They're not any happier than anybody else would be to be drafted, but I find the great majority feel they have an obligation to their country and are willing to accept it. Regardless of how they feel about being inducted, after six months they will be the finest soldiers—resourceful, brave, competent—able to carry out difficult assignments in a difficult war."

A Marine recruiting officer, himself a veteran of World War II and also Vietnam, voiced this compliment: "They're just as good as the Marines who were on Guadalcanal with me."

Boys Will Be Men

Charles M., nineteen, was a high school graduate and a warehouse manager when he received his induction notice.

"My wife doesn't like it," he said, "but she knows I have to leave. Everybody does in time of war. Nobody wants to go and fight, but you just have to."

Charles expressed a desire that they place him where they needed him most. When he gets out, he would like to have a training program in selling steel and aluminum supplies.

Jimmie S., twenty-two, was married and had a good job as therapist aid in a hospital.

"I don't mind it much," he said. "I didn't really want to go, but since I'm here, I'll make the best of it." He hopes to learn "some kind of trade" in the army, preferably welding.

Henry W., twenty-three, a college graduate, had been married two years. He wants to become a certified public accountant and hopes the army will assign him to a finance office or some administrative position. He feels that his leaving "is real rough" for his wife.

Mike G., a husky nineteen-year-old high school graduate, admitted that he was apprehensive. It bothered him that his girl friend and his parents were so broken up about his going. But "they figured it was his duty" and were beginning to accept it more cheerfully.

Mike worked as a dock hand for a motor freight line. Although he had intended to go to college, he just never had gotten started. Now, after the army, he plans to do so. "I'll be older and better able to do college work," he reasoned.

Jerry B., twenty, had been working in a machine shop but hopes after army service to join the state highway patrol. His leaving for the service will be hard on his family financially. He had been helping to support his mother and his brother and plans to send part of every paycheck home. He was asked to share his thoughts: "I just believe it's something we have to do," he replied. "I could have stayed out on a machinist deferment, but I thought I had an obligation to go in."

Leon L., twenty-four, is a high school graduate who had been working as a stock clerk. He expressed the hope that the army would send him to a data processing school.

"I'm not particularly sad about going in," he said. "I might get a good break out of it. It's all in the attitude you take toward it. I feel that it can be just like any other job. I plan to do my best."

Magnificent Morale

A chief medical officer, who was a resident in psychiatry before being called into army duty, reflected considerable satisfaction with his observations of these men.

"It was my impression as a civilian that there was generally a great deal of reluctance on the part of the fellows being inducted. However, I find quite the contrary. These boys, for the most part, are well motivated. Surprisingly few have significant personality problems which would interfere with their outlook towards serving their country. They appear to be accepting it. It's the exceptional fellow who determines to get out somehow."

The overwhelming majority of these young men have reflected a healthy, vigorous attitude. They look at their military service about like most adults look at paying their income tax. It is an obligation, a stake in a continuing America, and a contribution to the perpetuation of liberty in the life of man.

These young Americans were no more enthusiastic about Vietnam per se than the public generally. The issues have not been as clearly delineated as they were in World War II, and the lines are not as finely and blackly drawn. Nevertheless, they have responded with dedication, courage, and sometimes real enthusiasm!

Even among the men recovering from injuries sustained in

the current conflict morale runs unbelievably high. Very few complaints are heard in those hospital wards. They make it very clear that they have satisfied themselves as to the worthiness of their objective. And even though the price for them is great, they feel that it is worth the price.

One Negro soldier, in response to the question, "What would you like to do now?" answered, "Give me one good leg, and let me go back and help." He had no legs and was minus one arm, and he was very young. You get the distinct impression that some of these fellows regret that they have but one life to give to their country—and to the security of the free world!

A chaplain wrote: "I am now part of a military system engaged in the business of killing. It's a . . . . messy business. I hate it. I hate the whole idea of war. But this is something we have just plain got to do if we are to live in a free world."

He continued: "We soldiers know that killing is wrong. You don't need to tell us that. We do our utmost to make it as humane on civilians as we possibly can. But . . . . let's finish it as soon as we can."

The Only Alternative

Note the phrase, "if we are to live in a free world." He really believes that this is the only alternative. For him it has become black and white. The issues have fallen in place. He is sure where he stands.

Let no one accuse him of simply jumping to conclusions! He didn't. He measured the issues carefully and prayerfully. The probability is that it was not at all a black or white situation to begin with—it was a great mixture of greys. He did not attempt to escape the tension and the terror of the situation. He made no attempt to retreat "into the monastery," a neat little trick which characterized medieval religion. His dilemma was sharp, but he pondered its implications until the issue became clear. When he did decide, his decision was strong and resolute.

The Land I Love

Any American will be inspired by a review of the courageous and sacrificial actions of the fifty-six men who signed the Declaration of Independence. In fact, they didn't really sign it on the Fourth of July. They only *voted* to sign it. Then they got out of town because they had become traitors! They signed it a month later on August 2.

A price of five hundred pounds—a small fortune in those days—was placed on the heads of John Hancock and John Adams.

The names of those heroic Americans were not made public for six months in the hope that they could return home, establish refuge, and escape the ravages of the Crown. But some of them had a long way to go—all the way from New Hampshire to Georgia. And some never got back during all the years of the war. One who lived in New Jersey discovered when he returned home that his wife and some of his children had already been seized by the British and thrown into a dungeon.

They had pledged to give their "lives" and their "fortunes" if necessary in support of their declaration. Many of them lost both; most lost one or the other. The four New Yorkers who signed were all wealthy. Two of them had large fleets of ocean-sailing vessels. They lost everything, and all four died in sad circumstances.

They pledged their "sacred honor" and not a man wavered. They were true to their commitment. And their example has been a shining light for numerous men and women who have followed in their train.

In recent years it has become stylish to engage in free and unbridled criticism of our system of government. Of course, freedom guarantees the right to find fault as well as to give praise. But it seems that we have done this so loudly and persistently that many people outside have decided to believe it!

When we add to this the ugly caricature which some of our people have presented while visiting other countries and cultures, we should not be surprised to discover the disdain with which our citizenship is held in some places.

But that is the exception!

Generally, American citizenship is still respected and usually envied by the vast majority of other peoples in the world. The exception is the result of misunderstanding. We can safely assume that the fundamental principles of our government are sound and healthy. We can take great pride in the fact that we are indeed Americans!

We believe in America! We believe in her system of government. Imperfect as she is, her Bill of Rights guarantees to every man the right to his personal conscience and privacy in his own affairs. It guarantees to every man the right of trial by jury—admitting immediately that at best such procedures are performed by human beings. There is inevitably an occasional miscarriage of justice.

We cherish the economic principle of free enterprise, granting each person the privilege of earning the necessities for himself and his family. We cherish the freedom of speech and press which is so uniquely American.

We believe in the people of America. We are not all angels; neither are we all culprits. As a large and great nation, we have many misguided and irresponsible peoples within our ranks; but the ideals of the majority continue to sustain the upright and inspire the young. Our fathers did "bring forth on this continent a new nation, conceived in liberty and dedicated to the proposition that all men are created equal." We are enriched by their heritage and inspired by their example.

We believe in the God of America. We believe that our God is an international God—with his love reaching beyond the boundaries of all the nations of the earth. We believe that he is a God of moral justice and judgment. We believe, with President

Nixon, that our greatest problems today are fundamentally spiritual and that the source of help is in God.

We have been humbled by our national sins and perplexed by our internal disturbances. But we believe our cause is just and that adequate resources are within our reach. The sacrifices become insignificant when we properly appreciate the privilege of being an American.

Rights and Responsibilities

Citizenship is a term indicating the individual's relationship to the state. It comes from an old Latin word *civis,* denoting a person who enjoyed freedom. He was referred to as a free man. He enjoyed the public rights of voting and of holding and disposing of property. He was accorded the private rights of marriage and domestic relations. Of course, civil law provided the precepts and the conditions by which these rights could be exercised.

The term citizenship has maintained an aura of distinction and honor from ancient Rome onward. It has carried a connotation of great privileges and commensurate responsibilities. These two sides of our citizenship must be kept in mind as we place them in this particular context.

As Americans we have greater privileges than the citizens of ancient Rome ever dreamed of! Our responsibilities are correspondingly more grave.

Our government promises to secure and safeguard our inherent inalienable rights. It commits itself to the advancement of the welfare of its citizens. It attempts to maintain friendly relations with other nations in order to preserve and thus advance the general progress of mankind.

Seven basic civil liberties are guaranteed under our Constitution. They are:

(1) Freedom from unlawful restriction of the person
(2) Right of trial by jury

(3) Right of freedom of speech
(4) Freedom of worship
(5) Right of assembly
(6) Security of private property
(7) Equality of all persons before the law

These liberties are guaranteed in writing to all citizens of the United States, whether they are citizens by birth or by naturalization. Usually, as a matter of courtesy, they are extended also to aliens temporarily residing in this country.

It is axiomatic that people cannot enjoy such rights without assuming commensurate responsibilities. Citizens owe allegiance! We must recognize legally constituted authority. We must render such services as participation in courtroom procedures, paying taxes, and holding office.

Rights with Responsibilities

Citizens are expected to vote—and to take the time and trouble to prepare to vote intelligently. In case of national danger, citizens must render the military service necessary for the mutual interest. Such services are indispensable for the maintenance of stable government and the protection of our liberties. When we decline to assume these responsibilities, our own claims to the rights and privileges of our country are weakened.

There has been much resistance to the slogan, "Our country, right or wrong." It is substantially improved by the following reflection: "Our country, right or wrong. When right, to be kept right; when wrong, to be put right." George Linnaeus Banks in his poem "What I Live For" puts it this way:

> "For the cause that needs assistance,
> For the wrong that needs resistance,
> For the future in the distance,
> And the good that I may do."

Traitors and Malcontents

In recent years an increasing number of people have declined to carry their share of citizenship responsibilities. Many of them are lovable people personally, but they are confused, irresolute, and irresponsible. Some of them have failed in the primary commitments, and their lives have become a tangled web of compromise and deceit. They deceive themselves, their families, and the society in which they live.

It is sad to see them living off the accumulated legacies which others have won for them in the past. They take what they can from the social situation in which they live and put little or nothing back into it. They apparently assume that somebody else will work even harder and pay more dearly, thereby, compensating for their evasion and irresponsibility.

You can hear them on one hand damning the selfishness of other people; on the other hand, they openly assume these "selfish" people will become unselfish enough to give that "extra" to take care of the deadbeat and the freeloader.

Yet these people expect our statesmen to create peace on earth and good will to men! In many respects they are the real traitors to the race. They will tell you that they wouldn't harm a fly; but by their very withdrawal they become involved in the erosion and forfeiture of the very principles they claim to espouse.

Observers are convinced that if this trend continues they will not only make it difficult to conclude the present war—but they will make another war inevitable! For if peace is the fruit of righteousness, then war is certainly one of the fruits of indulgence. Those, who during a war effort, lie back and take it easy, play the black market, and thrive on others' misery, contribute to the decline of an economy which is already taxed to the limit.

Their pious words are hollow. The name of their game is indolence and indulgence. They are in consort with the enemy.

They need to be recognized for what they are: misguided, sick, sad, and lost! They are as dangerous to our free society as a footpad in the night, an arson-bug near a gas tank, or a maniac in an airplane.

We cannot avoid the issue. The battle rages. The war of ideas goes on. If we refuse to fight for liberty, some day we may find ourselves on the other side—fighting against it!

One of the multitudes of Unknown Soldiers left behind this witness:

"O weary world, open your ears to our cries that rise from beneath the sand and earth. We hated to die. There was so much we wanted yet to do. But for us, nothing can now be done. Only little white crosses and a woman's tears. But remember us and how dearly bought has been the liberty of which we so lightly boasted throughout our nation's life.

We are not heroes. We are just plain dead Americans. We died prematurely. We can only rest in peace if we can be sure that we have not died in vain."

The Strength of Youth

Without romanticizing war in the least, we must recognize the young men and women of high intelligence and sincere purpose who have gone forth inspired and supported by the noble ideals to which they were committed. They did not want to do what they had to do. They rose above everything selfish and endured, seeing the invisible, and everywhere they acquitted themselves with courage, patience, and faith.

A visitor to a veteran's hospital tried to sympathize with a soldier who had lost his leg, saying, "I am sorry you lost your leg." The lad replied, "I didn't lose it; I bought a clean conscience with it." It is good for us to think through that remark for it represents the thinking of thousands upon thousands of American youth who have won for us the right to be free!

We sometimes forget the capacities and accomplishments of

youth. Thomas Jefferson drafted the Declaration of Independence at thirty-three. Napoleon conquered Italy at twenty-five. Alexander the Great won most of his great military victories while still in his twenties. He founded the city of Alexandria when twenty-four.

Demosthenes was the greatest orator of Greece at twenty-five, and at the same age, Cicero was Rome's most eloquent speaker.

William Gladstone was a member of the British House of Commons at twenty-four, and Benjamin Franklin was writing articles for publication at fourteen.

Gibbon, the great English historian, was being published at twenty-four, and Ruskin was an accomplished art critic at the same age.

William Cullen Bryant wrote "Thanatopsis" at seventeen, Tennyson's first poems appeared at twenty, and Milton wrote one of his best poems at twenty-two.

Martin Luther was a professor of philosophy at twenty-four, and George Washington was mastering military strategy in his twenties.

More recent records are equally replete with the heroics of our nation's young. They continue to astound us with their feats in academics, athletics, business, and especially the military.

A twenty-five year old army captain wrote about those "magnificent" men who served under him:

"As I said a couple of times in my letters home, when you remember me in your prayers, remember to pray that I be given strength, character, and courage to lead these magnificent Americans. I say that in all sincerity, and I hope I have proved worthy of their faith, trust, and confidence."

At another time he wrote: "Through good fortune and the grace of God, I was chosen a leader—an honor that meant more to me than any of you will ever know. God alone knows how hard I have tried to make myself a worthy leader of these magnificent men! I feel so unworthy, at times, of the great trust my country and my fellow soldiers have put in me."

This fine American was killed in action, but his kind leave behind them a legacy which enriches and inspires us all.

A boy from North Carolina anticipated his death in Vietnam and composed a letter to his parents which was found among his personal effects after his death. Among other touching and clever expressions, he envisioned himself as presenting his credentials at the Gate of Heaven: "One more G.I. from Vietnam, St. Peter. I've served my time in Hell."

Then he added: "Don't mourn for me, Mother, for I'm happy I died fighting for my country's enemies, and I will live forever in peoples' minds. I've done what I've always dreamed of . . . I died a soldier of the United States of America. God bless you all and take care. I'll be seeing you in Heaven."

Vietnam – A Symbol

August 4, 1964, is a date which may loom large in the history books of future generations. On that night in the Tonkin Gulf, two U. S. destroyers were steaming around in international waters about sixty miles off the coast of Vietnam. Communist gun boats suddenly initiated an attack by torpedo and gun fire.

Two days earlier some shots had been aimed at the *Maddox* and the *Turner Joy*. Our government warned the attackers not to do it again. But they did.

Two versions of the incident emerged in Washington. In the mind of Senator Fulbright, Foreign Relations Committee chairman, the event may have been nothing more than the exaggerated or even imagined "incident" which incumbent President Johnson needed for campaign purposes. In the suspected hyperbole of the Defense Department, the assault was premeditated and preplanned.

Other observers compare the Tonkin incident with the sinking of the armored cruiser *Maine* on February 15, 1898. It went down with the loss of 260 lives in the Havana harbor, and constituted the "incident" that set off the Spanish-American War.

People still argue as to whether the blowing up of the *Maine* came from an internal bomb or an external torpedo. A hundred years from now a similar debate may still be going on as to what really happened that night in the Tonkin Gulf. Both incidents are shrouded in "classified" categories and the responsible authorities are very properly protective of the literal facts.

The United States' response to the Communist attack was dramatic. Planes were ordered from the aircraft carriers *Ticonderoga* and *Constellation* to bomb the Communist mainland. Congress immediately passed the Gulf of Tonkin resolution which put us into undeclared war against the Hanoi government.

Some political observers were suspicious that the campaigning President had made political capital of the entire matter. His opponent, Barry Goldwater, had charged the Democrats with enacting another Bay of Pigs. Suddenly, however, Mr. Johnson had struck the enemy in what appeared to be justified retaliation. His previous image of a "peace" candidate now gave way to one who could move effectively in defense of American lives and property!

In retrospect, it is quite clear that the President could have done no less—but he could well have done much more. We were already in a shooting war with the Communists in South Vietnam (just as in the 1890's we were on the doorstep of a war with Spain) before the dramatic confrontation. But right or wrong, the United States did not proceed in strength as we did three-quarters of a century earlier.

The Unpopular War

Its staunchest supporters have never claimed that the Vietnam war was popular. Such a lack of enthusiasm is not really surprising. A jungle boobytrap ten thousand miles away is not considered an ideal place for an American boy to die. And the primitive aspects of the field operation have revived our repugnance.

We have never before fought a war like this on so massive a scale. Obviously it has not submitted to conventional military planning. The political implications were inextricably bound up with strategy and tactics. Every move had to be calculated with the highest possible sensitivity projection.

Many authorities contended that the war was impossible to win and too costly to pursue. Some who conceded the probability that we could prevent a Viet Cong take-over expressed grave doubt that we could establish a stable, independent, noncommunist government.

So it is claimed that the United States simply walked into a political trap in Vietnam! And it was proposed that the sooner we got out the better! The costs and risks were seen to be out of proportion to the most favorable success in our objectives.

After five years of involvement and gradual escalation, the objections reached crescendo proportions in the mid-sixties. When asked why we were there in the first place we said it was because we were committed to the right of the South Vietnamese to self-determination; our adversary countered with the charge that we were interfering with that right!

Was it our duty and in our national interest to set ourselves to the containment of Communism in Asia? Was Vietnam the right place and was war the right way to "contain" it? Just how much substance was there in the suggestion that if South Vietnam were to fall to the Communists all of Southeast Asia would follow? Who was the real enemy: The Communist-controlled National Liberation Front of South Vietnam, North Vietnam, or the Communist regime in Peking? To what degree were we risking war with China and/or the Soviet Union?

Some who had approved of our original involvement suddenly switched. But this raised a further question. Had we now made commitments which we could break only at the sacrifice of our prestige, our moral standing as a nation, and our credibility as an ally to the other peace-loving nations of the world?

The debate raged on all aspects of the conflict: its causes, its tactics, its ultimate purposes. The pros and cons were advanced in Congress, in academia, the church, and the cocktail party.

We began to talk about "hawks" and "doves"—terms of limited usefulness because again absolute identification and definition are so difficult to come by.

The Congress was divided. But the hawks and the Administration-oriented middle group were in the vast majority. Outside Congress the most articulate doves were found among leftists, pacifists, clergymen, civil rights leaders, and the academic community. Our entire foreign policy and our policy on Vietnam in particular, was evaluated, discussed, argued and reviewed—as perhaps never before in the history of mankind.

Whatever our original commitments meant to us, it became crystal clear that they were accepted by a succession of Saigon regimes as an earnest of our determination to support them against Communist aggression. Hundreds of thousands of South Vietnamese committed themselves to the anti-communist cause as a result of our encouragement and identification.

Hawks and Doves

Some object to our involvement in Vietnam as purely political. Others object on moral and religious grounds. Obviously, some observers and authorities represent a combination of both kinds of concern.

Some believe that our presence there was a clear violation of the Geneva Agreement of 1954. They are also embarrassed that we became identified with the rule of President Diem, who was finally exposed as a harsh, autocratic leader hated by his own people.

Many people believe that our tactics in Vietnam are inappropriate and unsuccessful. We were obviously unprepared to retaliate effectively in a guerrilla style war. They contend that our techniques of mass destruction and "scorched-earth policies" are indefensible—that this type of military victory is a political and moral defeat!

The point is made that although we went there in the interest of the Vietnamese themselves, our larger interest was really our own welfare. The question emerges as to whether it was right for us to fight our battle on their land! We were reminded that "our helpfulness may leave Vietnam a scarred blot on Asia and at the same time further alienate us from friend and foe alike.

Critics believe that our persistence in Vietnam has tarnished the image of the United States as a law-abiding and peace-loving nation. In the eyes of many other nations of the world the United States appears to be a bully, slaughtering innocent people in an effort to make our own point. There is even some concern about our continuing relationship to Japan. Extending beyond our allies and neutral powers, this concern applies to our relations with communist nations. It is feared that our relationship to Russia is being adversely affected. And obviously the wedge between China and the United States is being driven even deeper.

But those, who have so often accused the Administration of insincerity and phoniness, have themselves been terribly vulnerable. They have demonstrated closed minds and unbelievable inflexibility, and they have often refused to listen to the other side! Some of their spokesmen and writers are so committed to a doctrinaire position that one is able to predict in advance, far in advance, what they will say and how they will stand on the related issues of the day.

In the early stages of the student uprisings in Berkeley, California, a young woman whose father has been a leader in the Communist party, and who is herself an avowed Communist, marched with many others about the White House chanting, "The President doesn't give a . . . about what is happening in Vietnam." Most of us resent both what she said and the way she said it. But she was simply being more blunt than most of the activistic and militant doves.

From the right, came arrogant demands that the U. S. bomb North Vietnam's ports, dams, and people. "You are not fighting

human beings over there," one of them declared. "You're just
fighting two-legged animals. The people are just slaves."

On the left, the anti-war demonstrators matched these hawkish and intemperate tirades—and far surpassed them in volume!
Washington marchers left the Pentagon Mall in disarray after a
sordid and disgustingly obscene camp-in. At Baltimore's Selec-
tive Service Office, a Roman Catholic priest and two laymen
poured two pints of blood over sixteen file drawers of records
while a Protestant minister stood look-out. All four were ar-
rested for their misguided enthusiasm and charged with mutilat-
ing public records.

In 1968 a Dartmouth College valedictorian urged his classmates to refuse to fight in Vietnam. "Thank God, we are losing
that war," he shouted, and was given a standing ovation by his
classmates. But parents and alumni stood up and yelled,
"Shame," "Traitor," and other expressions of disagreement.

Clergy and Church Divided

Various religious personalities and publications have labeled
the Vietnam war "clearly immoral." They have even urged
young men to decline participation because of the conflicts
involved. Some have devised techniques of protest through civil
disobedience and tax refusal. Others derided and discredited
these sentiments.

One national Negro group passed a resolution condemning
our actions while another with a membership of more than five
million voted its approval of the way President Johnson was
handling the conflict. Roman Catholics saw Cardinal Spellman
expressing openly his support of the Johnson Administration
while Monsignor Sheen made a trip to the White House to beg
the President to withdraw the troops!

A Southern Baptist editor called for the withdrawal while a
brash young denominational officer in Florida suggested that we
"bomb the . . . ." out of North Vietnam—claiming that to be

the only language the Communists could understand. National surveys have reflected similar divisions within the laity.

Returns indicate that those persons who are considered "conservative" theologically tend to be hawkish and "liberal" Christians tend toward the dove position. Some Christian leaders speak so hawkishly that one has difficulty understanding what Christian love has ever meant to them. Others seem to want to compromise so quickly one wonders if they understand the implications of peace at any price. The Christian gospel is deserving of more responsible examples—on both sides!

Upon returning (in 1968) from his third trip to Vietnam, Rear Admiral James W. Kelly, outlined the general feeling of military personnel who have been involved. Chaplain Kelly affirmed that there was a "deep religious concern on the part of our people in Vietnam." He said that in his twenty-six years of experience in the military he had never seen such mature concern expressed with such depth.

He named (1) a God-centered morality about our involvement, (2) a conviction that "we are in the right place to preserve the peace in the world," and (3) that the principle is worth the price.

Our missionaries in the area echo similar sentiments. It should be remembered that they are there by choice—they were not conscripted. They are also free to think for themselves and to form opinions and judgments regarding their involvement in South Vietnamese life and thought.

The pastor of Saigon's Trinity Baptist Church serves as a sort of supervisor of Southern Baptist Missionary work in the Saigon area. He spoke for himself and his fellow missionaries: "We strongly feel that the people of South Vietnam need to have the right of freedom of choice. We are willing to give our lives alongside of American servicemen if necessary to guarantee this right."

He stated that people there were "hungry for the gospel," and

that without American help their needs could not be met. He
also ventured the opinion that without American help Communism would take the country, Asia, and the rest of the world!

Another missionary said, "It is difficult for me to understand
how Christians could be against what the United States is doing
in Vietnam. If we left . . . the Communists would take over,
and the privilege of preaching the gospel ends. What happened
in China demonstrates that."

He said without equivocation that "when you've lived under
the shadow of Communism as much as we have, I cannot
conceive of our pulling out." His wife is confident that her
husband reflects the feeling of every missionary in Vietnam.

Each individual citizen has the moral obligation to follow the
dictates of his conscience. This is a part of our freedom. We
must, however, make every effort to use this freedom constructively and responsibly. The behavior of some of our people has
undoubtedly given the enemy encouragement and hope, thereby
prolonging the war, causing greater losses to our own fighting
men, and possibly creating a temporary tactical disadvantage.
Careless behavior on the part of knowledgeable persons can
inspire similar behavior by other groups who are not nearly so
knowledgeable. Each successive step contributes to lawlessness
and disorder.

Background for Vietnam

The conditions in the world at the end of World War II set
the stage for United States prestige and responsibility in international affairs. Our country enjoyed a position of great strength,
both militarily and economically. Conversely, the rest of the
world had been greatly weakened by the war. Our country's new
role of world leadership was obvious to all and accepted by
most.

One by one the European powers abandoned their colonial
possessions, leaving great holes in the former power structure

such as that in Southeast Asia. Meanwhile, the Soviet Union was aggressively threatening not only Europe but Asia. Our former European allies were too weak to offer much resistance. The United Nations was too young and too weak to meet the crisis. The United States felt constrained by conscience and the pressure of her allies to assume the role of leadership in the world which time and circumstance now dictated. This, in itself, involved our nation in Southeast Asian affairs and particularly in Vietnam which was ripe for Communism after the French withdrawal.

The victory of Communism in China in 1949 created a situation in Asia which was as ominous as that which prevailed in Europe. South Korea was immediately invaded. Under the supervision of the United Nations, the United States, with the assistance of a few allies, sent resources and personnel to take "police action."

The result was something less than a military victory in the customary use of the term, but it did prevent a Communist take-over of South Korea. It also demonstrated that the free world would not tolerate continued Communist tactics in such invasion procedures in weaker nations.

When France relinquished her claims in 1954, Indo-China was divided into four parts; Cambodia, Laos, North Vietnam, and South Vietnam. The division of Vietnam at the seventeenth parallel represented a concession to Communist claims on the North and declared for South Vietnam the right of self-determination with the guarantee of popular participation in the forth-coming general elections.

When the Geneva Accords were drawn in 1954, it appeared that Hanoi expected all of South Vietnam to fall to Communism within a short time. There is even the supposition that they agreed to the Accords for that very reason. After all, they had army personnel strategically planted in the south, weapons concealed, and a definite plan to undermine the new government there. The strategy was assassination of leaders and general terrorism.

Eighty thousand South Vietnamese soldiers who had been fighting in the army had been ordered to the North for training in the army for what had now become North Vietnam. These men were to become known as the Viet Cong and would return to South Vietnam to begin the conquest. The fact that so many of them were native southerners led to the charge that the war was a revolution rather than an invasion.

Cold War Gets Hot

In September of 1960, the Communist Party of North Vietnam in its Third Party Congress created the National Liberation Front, the political organization for directing the guerrilla war in the south. From that moment on the infiltration of the south was aggressively pursued. The Viet Cong conscripted young men from the villages and countryside and by persuasion or absolute force, formed the guerrilla units which waged the war.

As the reservoir of southern-born Viet Cong forces ran low, North Vietnamese soldiers began to appear in the southern struggle. This infiltration took place at night and in secret but regular army units from the north suddenly began to appear in regimental strength in the south! The terrorists assassinated hundreds of local government officials and kidnapped hundreds of others while armed guerrillas killed and injured thousands of military and security personnel.

The Communist assault on South Vietnam led to a request for help, and the United States was one of several nations which gave ready response. We shared in the responsibility as advisors, suppliers, and participants. Then North Vietnamese torpedo boats attacked our destroyers in the Gulf of Tonkin, and the situation became extremely critical.

On August 10, 1964, the United States Senate voted eighty-eight to two to support the previous commitments made to

South Vietnam; the House approved four hundred sixteen to nothing. From that moment, the advisors became combatants and more and more of the war effort was assumed by United States military forces.

We became involved in Vietnam not for profit but for principle. As a nation we did not want one inch of Vietnamese soil. We had no interest in annexing the country as a colony. We simply responded to an SOS!

We were motivated by several factors. Of prime significance was an awareness that a takeover of two hundred million persons in the nations of Southeast Asia could constitute a serious shift in the balance of power and the position of strength of the free world allies. It was with profound regret and excruciating agony that we became more and more deeply involved. But we stood behind the commitments which we had made.

"Containment" of Communism

The Vietnam conflict is really a symbol of world tension between two diametrically opposed systems of government and ways of life. We hope and pray that these two worlds may coexist in peace. However, when one tries to overrun the other, it is only natural and right that the other should defend itself and protect its way of life.

In recent years we have generally followed a "containment policy" designed to prevent the spread of Communism in places like Berlin, Lebanon, Greece, the Dominican Republic, Cuba —and Vietnam. We believe that if we fail to curb the spread in Vietnam, this sinister force will finally conquer Southeast Asia, Indonesia, the Philippines, and Australia. By fighting now to stop the spread, we are preventing worse trouble in the years to come.

We admit that coexistence is tentative and uncertain with such a philosophy. The word "peace" has one meaning to the Communist spokesman and an entirely different meaning to the democracies. To most Communists it seems to be the kind of peace which the canary has made with the cat. It appears that only one kind of peace will ever satisfy the most aggressive Communist leaders: that is the peace of the tyrant that has crushed all his opposition under his iron heel.

When Vietnam is settled, the struggle will shift, but it will continue. Previously it was Korea, and next it may be Laos. But the basic issue is more ideological than political. Once we understand this it will be easier for us to grasp the implications of the current situation and proceed with preventive and corrective strategies for the future.

Summary

Most of us recognize the nuclear implications if the Vietnam conflict were to escalate into World War III. At the same time, we are frightened at the prospect of Communist expansion in Southeast Asia. The modern Russian version of Communism is less frightening to us than the "mad dog" brand represented by the Chinese-Cuban-Asian pattern. At best, however, it poses an avowed threat to religious and political freedom.

The vast majority of Christians, along with an apparent majority of non-Christian leaders of the free world, are committed to some kind of effort which would avoid both of these undesirable alternatives. A continuation of our "limited objectives" policy is clearly a lesser evil than either of the other two. Such policy commits us to a persistence which will communicate our strength and our political intent. Clearly understood, this warns the enemy that he can never win! At the same time, it requires enough restraint to assure both friend and foe that we seek no advantage of our own.

Is War Glorious?

A renowned lecturer once said to a high school student body, "Every nation needs a good war about once every thirty years." Such a sentiment is consistent with ancient tradition and perhaps with general opinion. Even Shakespeare's *Othello* talked about the "pride, pomp and circumstance of glorious war." And Wilhelm von Humboldt said that the effect of war upon national character is "one of the most salutary elements in the molding of the race."

If, however, you try telling that to some G.I. fresh from Vietnam, his response would not likely be quotable in *The Ladies Home Journal!* We share his deep and burning resentment of such buffoonery and irresponsibility. We are compelled to consider the counsel of others.

Sherman said, "War is hell." Franklin D. Roosevelt said, "I hate war." Dwight D. Eisenhower said sadly, "May God deliver us from another world war!" Arnold Toynbee, the English historian, declares that today war "is the crucial question on which the destiny of our civilization hangs." Emil Brunner, the late Swiss theologian, speaking of war, says, "We are here confronted by one of the most controversial ethical problems of the present day." The new dimensions of war with the threat of thermonuclear annihilation, have caused one writer to call it "thinking about the unthinkable."

General John J. Pershing said, "Unless civilization destroys

35

war, war will destroy civilization." President John F. Kennedy paraphrased the same sentiment: "Mankind must put an end to war or war will put an end to mankind."

We will make a giant step forward in the achievement of this global objective when we determine to tell the truth about war. We must take away all the glamour, all the chivalry, and all the romanticism that misguided generations have associated with it. We must learn to tell the truth—the unvarnished truth about war!

We are not suggesting the exposure of intelligence or reconnaissance activities. It is unthinkable that coded and classified information be made public. The national interest and our hemispheric security are dependent upon such elaborate and extensive confidence files.

We simply need to maintain perspective about the havoc and horror of military conflict. No matter how fully justified it may seem, it shatters homes and produces unnumbered orphans and widows. It always brings some dislocation, destruction, and human despair. The misery and calamity of war stalk abroad like specters over the face of the earth. We can even hear the voices from the grave crying aloud:

> "If ye who live
>   Break faith with us who die
>   We will not sleep, though poppies grow
>   In Flanders field."

The History of War

War has been the prevailing mood in the history of man. From 1496 B.C. to A.D. 1861, the world has seen 227 years of peace and 3130 years of war. In the last 400 years, European nations have entered into more than 8,000 treaties of peace. They were intended to remain in force forever. They have lasted, on an average, for only two years!

The frequency of war is absolutely astounding. From 500

B.C. to A.D. 1924, we have records on 967 major conflicts in the history of Greece, Rome, Austria, Germany, England, France, the Netherlands, Spain, Italy, Russia, Poland, and Lithuania. These wars have occurred on an average of one every two- and one-half-years.

Periods of peace as long as a quarter of a century have been exceedingly rare in the world's history.

All this time, cruelties and barbarities have steadily increased. Armies have grown bigger and bigger. Weapons have become more and more terrible. And at each stage, more and more of the world population has become involved.

In the United States no generation has been free from war. Our country has engaged in nine major conflicts since 1776, for an average of one every twenty-five years. The present war in Vietnam may continue for many years, while other so-called wars of national liberation may break out in Southeast Asia, Latin America, or Africa at any time.

In World War I, the allies and central powers mobilized a total of 65,038,810 men. Of that number, 8,538,315 gave their lives. The combined casualties including the wounded and missing totaled 37,508,686.

World War II resulted in the fantastic death toll of 22,000,000 of the world's finest men and women. It left another 34,400,000 wounded. It is impossible to estimate the toll in property, interrupted education, warped attitudes, and hateful inclinations.

The suicidal dimensions of war are suggested by the old limerick about the two cats of Kilkenny:

> Each thought there was one cat too many;
> So they fought and they spit,
> And they scratched and they bit,
> 'Till, excepting their nails
> And the tips of their tails,
> Instead of two cats, there weren't any.

General Dwight Eisenhower said, "War is the greatest of social diseases." General Douglas MacArthur made a sweeping indictment of war when he said, "With today's weapons there is no longer any advantage to winning a war. Everybody loses, with the victor only losing a little less than the vanquished." General H. H. Arnold supported this view: "One nation cannot defeat another nation today. That concept died with Hiroshima. War is like fire; you can prevent a fire or you can try to put it out, but you can't win a fire because fire is destruction." General Omar Bradley vows that "the only way to win an atomic war is to make certain it never starts."

Old Pyrrhus of Epirus said: "One more such victory and Pyrrhus will be no more." Little by little we are beginning to recognize the prophetic truth of his statement. Preoccupation with war, with the irrational hysteria which accompanies every international incident, could, at any moment, make his observation truly prophetic for our time. Our world is threatened, as it has never been threatened before, with dictators and totalitarian regimes. Yet we fought and we won a war to "make the world safe for democracy." We fought and won a "war to end all wars."

Removing the Mask

We must tell the truth about the ultimate futility of force in the affairs of man. War never shows who is wrong; it only shows who is strong. There was a time when a man got his wife by force and held her by force. There was a time when labor was compelled to work by force; a time when prisoners were dealt with solely by force. There was a time when children were compelled to do their tasks under the threat of physical punishment. But that time has passed! The folly, the fallacy, and the futility of force have been revealed. A "war to crush militarism" brought on more militarism. The "war for democracy" established several dictators.

There was a time when men fought one another in the duel. There was a day when families fought one another in the family feud. Clan fought against clan, tribe against tribe, city against city, and state against state. With humanity's slow and painful progress, these patterns of conflict have been almost completely eliminated. Yet, nation still fights against nation.

Even in the animal kingdom force does not prevail. Witness the fate of the dinosaur, the glyptodont, the mastodon and other mighty animals of antiquity. They were large and powerful, equipped for offense and defense with magnificent scales and claws. But they no longer exist. We would no longer know of them were it not for our museums of natural history.

Force alone is inadequate. Force breeds suspicion. Suspicion breeds isolation. And isolation breeds extinction. Mere physical force without moral force makes for suicide and self-annihilation.

The Biological Truth

The evolutionary process is a matter of primary and continuing concern to mankind. To assure the continuing improvement of the species is an objective of mutual interest and import.

But who goes to war? Flat-footed people? No. Nearsighted people? No. Morons, epileptics, degenerates? No. They are not good enough. They are left behind to become the fathers of the next generation. The strong, the sturdy, the sensitive and intelligent, are sent forth to be sacrificed on the altar of war! Yet the humblest farmer knows full well that you can't improve a breed of hogs like that. He can tell you very quickly that no one can improve a herd of cows with such irresponsible selectivity.

The biological truth about war uncovers a principle in human society which is one and the same. In fact, the Napoleonic Wars produced a specific historical example: The qualifications for soldiers had to be gradually reduced. This was necessary, at least physically speaking, because an inferior type of human being had arrived on the scene. The generation was weakened, and it took several decades to accomplish any appreciable recovery. And there is no way of measuring the moral decay.

The Sociological Truth

So long as we are willing to spend huge sums of money to wage wars but reluctant to spend similar sums to rehabilitate ghettos and relieve poverty, we are not telling the whole truth!

Three months before World War I, David Lloyd George said to the people of England: "Give me two hundred million dollars and I shall blot out the poverty of England. I shall do away with the social maladjustments. I shall stamp out disease. I shall open recreation centers. I shall make of England a garden of Eden."

The next morning every newspaper in Great Britain, and nearly every newspaper in America, carried a front page cartoon of David Lloyd George with his finger pointed to his forehead. They accused him of being a traitor. They vowed that such foolhardy plans would bankrupt the British Empire. Some said he was a dreamer; others called him utopian, and others branded him simply as an idealist. They were unanimous in saying that such fantastic sums of money could not be obtained.

But three months passed. Suddenly Great Britain was spending two hundred million dollars. Monies were spent not to stamp out poverty and do away with disease, not to alleviate social maladjustments; not to build hospitals, educational institutions and recreation centers; not once and for all for constructive social purposes! But Great Britain spent two hundred million dollars every week for fifty-two weeks each year, for four-and-a-half long years—to kill, maim and mutilate, to multiply widows and orphans and to bring sorrow, destitution, and misery to untold millions of homes!

Our own nation is experiencing great stress and strain on this issue. The war on poverty has been curtailed by the escalating costs of our Vietnam involvement. Some of the Great Society programs have been shelved in favor of the war effort. Monies unobtainable for social reform have been commandeered for the military!

The Moral Truth

A few months ago, a young sergeant was preparing to return to his home after serving a tour of active duty at an army post in the Vietnam theatre. Two years before, his national guard unit had been mobilized, and he had left his wife and children to go overseas. Though he had never seen combat, this sergeant was a war casualty. His skin had never been torn by hostile metal, but his moral character had been disfigured and his soul had been scarred. He had surrendered to the temptations so familiar to the military and so predictable under conditions of extreme loneliness, frustration, and futility.

Now the prospect of reunion with his beloved family made him desperately ashamed and afraid. He sat on his footlocker in the barracks and talked with uninhibited honesty to his chaplain. How could he face his wife again? He had been unfaithful to her. He had stooped to awful sin. He was sad and sorry. His body was sick, and his soul was sad. His shoulders were slumped, and his conversation was coarse and callous. He knew that within a month he would have to begin a new life, and he didn't see how he would ever be able to do it!

In our evaluation of the effects of war, we must be willing to admit that there are many who are afraid to go home again! Military experience has left many more casualties than those recorded in the records of the Pentagon or marked by a white cross in Arlington Cemetery! The casualty lists of modern armies are not completed with the mention of the dead and wounded who have fallen in battle. Unrecorded and sometimes forgotten is the injury to moral character which accompanies every military operation.

Fortunately, many individuals remain pure even when confronted by seemingly overwhelming temptation. Some men in military life have drawn so adequately from the spiritual resources of our faith that they have been able to bear a striking witness to both their buddies and civilians. But these appear to be the exception. It is terribly hard to remain clean, upright, and exemplary midst all of the contrary pressures which war symbolizes.

Who then would presume to estimate the permanent effect of war upon the participants? How do you go about measuring the damage to the surviving soldiers—especially the combat veterans? What happens to the mind and spirit of a man when he is taught to kill? How can we possibly forget this awful facet of truth about war?

Here is a typical portion of an address delivered by a World War II army officer training a group of boys in a bayonet drill. The major emphasized that it was a good thing to show each G.I. how to kill the enemy. He explained his objective in getting them to feel at home with the instrument of death in their hand —and to remember that it was there to kill!

"You've got to get down and hook them out with a bayonet; you will enjoy that, I assure you. Get sympathy out of your head. We go out to kill. We don't care how so long as they are killed. And I say to you, if you see a wounded German, shove him out and have no nonsense about it! Kill them, every mother's son of them. Remember that your job is to kill—that is the only way—exterminate the vile creatures. . . . I remember a corporal saying to me, pointing to some German prisoners close by, 'Can I do these blokes in, Sir?' I said, 'Please yourself.' He did. When the corporal came back he said, 'I felt something that I have never felt before. . . . I felt what it is like to kill; but it's . . . hard to get it out. . . . He had a belly like iron!' "

It is no wonder that some people believe sincerely that the declaration of war is an abrogation of morality; that war is a moratorium on morality. They see war as a desecration of every one of the Ten Commandments. For example, it desecrates the Second Commandment because it is a worship of a false god—the god of war. War abuses the Third Commandment because the name of God is taken in vain; the Fourth because the Sabbath cannot be hallowed by bloodshed and mass murder; the Fifth because parents are dishonored by the destruction of their offspring.

"Thou shalt not kill" is disavowed and denied; "Thou shalt not commit adultery" falls victim to wartime situation ethics; "Thou shalt not steal" is ignored and forgotten in the territorial take-over which so frequently motivates war in the first place. The command against "bearing false witness" is terribly hard to reconcile with the common patterns of propaganda; and "Thou shalt not covet" is frequently the cause of the whole . . . business in the first place!

The Truth About the Untruth

The "credibility gap" of our current national situation is not at all unique in history. Our present leaders are not significantly different from their predecessors. They are neither much better nor much worse than previous wartime personnel. Wars are not fought with truth. They both result in and are produced by a process of falsification and distortion. Wars are fought under a smokescreen of clever and deliberate propaganda!

When the entire nation is organized for military engagement the question of "morale" is of great importance. People must be brought to believe that the war is necessary for the general welfare. We, therefore, resort to ingenious methods of propaganda to build up morale. Many types of influence and persuasion are used to induce every citizen to perform his part.

War propaganda always has a tendency to obscure the facts, arouse hatred, and make it generally difficult for the citizen to think clearly and sanely on the issues at stake. Even when the information is fundamentally factual, the psychological pressures of wartime are too great for most people to resist. They are caught up in the "spell." It is this feature of modern warfare which makes it even more vicious than that of earlier centuries. It tends to manipulate people, distort their visions, and destroy their ideals.

During wartime we tend to believe the most fantastic stories about the misbehavior and misdeeds of our enemies. For example, during the Spanish-American War, most Americans accepted without question the lurid tales about the Spaniards raping and torturing Cubans whom they had imprisoned in concentration camps. Similarly, during World War I, many Americans honestly believed that the German army occupying Belgium amused themselves by cutting off the hands of little children. During World War II we actually began to believe the propaganda line that "the only good Jap is a dead Jap."

Reflective objectivity makes it difficult to believe that we could have been willing—even eager—to believe such absurdly disparaging stories regarding our antagonists! It is, however, but a reflection of the extremes to which men will go in order to prime the emotional pump for the waging of war. We must understand that the wartime picture we held of our adversaries was frequently erroneous; the postwar attitudes which we found so surprising were really a return to the objectivity of emotional normalcy. Wars cannot be fought without falsehood. Every nation deliberately lies about the enemy nations.

In 1928 a little book appeared that was packed with dynamite. *Falsehood in Wartime* is the title, and it was written by Arthur Ponsonby, a member of the British House of Lords. It is a calm, dispassionate study of the so-called atrocities of the first World War. One after another most of them are shown to have been false. Such stories as "The Crucified Canadian," "The Corpse Factory" and the one about the cutting off of babies' hands are all shown to be the work of clever propagandists.

Fabrications and falsehoods are a most important part of war. The best minds available are commandeered for this phase of the war effort and enormous sums of money are expended. It is usually impossible for the average citizen to know where the propaganda ends and the truth begins.

It is a matter of record that at the close of one of our nation's wars a Washington official admitted that most of the atrocity stories that had been reported through the press and emphasized in pulpits had been manufactured by himself, sitting at his desk in the propaganda offices of the District of Columbia.

Many other illustrations of American wartime aberrations can be cited. For example, some of our most responsible people denounced everything remotely related to German or Japanese culture. They refused to read books written by German authors or to listen to music by German composers. They have even changed the names of streets so as to eliminate any trace of hostile associations.

It is not now necessary to whitewash the atrocities of the enemy. The record has been written. We can, however, insist that the facts be kept in perspective. Many Americans who visited Japan prior to that war know very well that there were thousands upon thousands of good citizens whose motives were unquestioned. They were caught in the grip of the irresistible power of their military and political leaders. Our missionaries were appalled and unconvinced by the blanket accusations of the propaganda machines.

Similarly, many of us made the mistake of believing that Germans were all like Hitler. We reasoned: Hitler is a German; Hitler is a bad man; therefore, all Germans are bad men! War hysteria gathered such momentum that we believed the worst.

We know now that millions of innocent Germans were thrust into the German war machine against their will. Some of them were bitterly opposed to Hitler but to refuse him meant certain death. False propaganda in the German educational system was so effective that the warped minds of German youth fell under the unbelievable spell of their Fuehrer. Those who dared challenge and question the trend were executed.

In the same manner, we tend to become blinded to the many faults of our allies. We "con" ourselves into believing that they can do no wrong. There were, therefore, millions of confused Americans when our relations with Russia did such a "flip-flop" following World War II.

The Political Truth

On February 15, 1898, the armored cruiser, *Maine,* was sunk in Havana harbor with the loss of two-hundred-sixty lives. It was the "incident" that set off the Spanish-American War. To this day, we don't know whether the blowing up of the *Maine* came from an internal bomb or an external torpedo. From time to time there are suspicions that rulers and leaders of nations make political capital out of such single incidents.

In 1952, at a press conference, President Truman said, "My greatest desire is to bring peace to the world." The President's declaration, however, was greeted with some suspicion. People remembered that in modern times every head of state who had started a war insisted that he was for peace!

Isolationists began to accuse President Truman of promoting the war in Korea in order to stay in office. They dubbed it "Truman's War." The charge at first fell on deaf ears. Republicans stood with Democrats in sustaining the President's determined efforts to uphold the United Nations in its policy of resistance to aggression. Finally, however, further questions and suspicions were entertained by responsible men. The casualties came in, and the costs of men and money mounted to staggering proportions. A sharp division arose over the dismissal of General MacArthur. Finally, the Korean intervention turned out to be very unpopular and became a leading issue in the 1952 presidential campaign.

We remember, also, that criticism arose from those who feared a depression. They argued that a war economy gives industrial bankers a chance to go all out for production. This naturally inflates wages and in turn, raises prices. The inevitable result is abnormal prosperity. War economy is a politician's delight as long as it lasts. Inflation inevitably subsides, however, and depression sets in. It is a heavy price to pay for temporary success. This was charged with vehemence by the Republicans in 1952.

The Cuban crisis illustrated the inclination of mankind to play politics with war. Without ever going so far as to advocate an armed attack on Cuba, some Congressmen made charges which could have had no result other than war if they had proved true. The obvious theme of the charges, which the Defense Department disproved, was plainly political. Occasional charges and counter charges in the same vein continued into the campaign season of 1964 and proved an embarrassment to the Republican as well as to the Democratic Party. They contributed, unfortunately, to American disquiet and disunity in a stormy world.

It appears that those Americans, in and out of Congress, who are tempted to play politics with war, are lacking in sufficient moral sensitivity concerning the role of truth in such a time as ours. Their minds must have been conditioned in the prenuclear era in which sane men could espouse a doctrine called "total war." That idea, dominant between 1914 and 1945, committed the total resources of men and material of one nation in a mobilized effort to destroy all the persons and properties of the enemy nation. This was considered to be a source which could be mobilized, rationed, and ruthlessly used as human cannon fodder.

Senator Barry Goldwater kept harping on our "no-win policy," apparently incapable of seeing any intermediate position between total war and total defeat. (We must understand that there is an intermediate position—one which provides for the survival of people and social systems on both sides. But this position itself is endangered when the politicians use the war issue as an instrument of intimidation, threat, or rabble-rousing.) At any rate Mr. Goldwater got a response to his challenge.

After the Gulf of Tonkin attack, the President ordered planes from the aircraft carriers, *Ticonderoga* and *Constellation,* to bomb the Communist mainland. He also took political action by asking Congress to pass his Gulf of Tonkin Resolution, which put us into undeclared war against the Hanoi government.

Whether it ever crossed his mind or not, the President, by this action, trumped the only ace that his campaigning opponent may have had up his sleeve. No longer could the Republican candidate charge the Democrats with enacting another Bay of Pigs. President Johnson had struck the enemy in what appeared to be justified retaliation. He had showed himself a "peace" candidate who could reluctantly but decisively make war in defense of American lives and property. True, we were already in a shooting war with Communists in South Vietnam, just as in the 1890's we were on the doorstep of war with Spain before the dramatic moment came. The main difference is that we didn't follow through in the twentieth century as we did in the nineteenth!

We like to believe that the men whom we elect to public office, and those whom we encourage to run, are men of moral responsibility. They will exercise deliberate restraint because of their love for their country. They are also men who are quite sensitive to the possibility of offending the electorate. In the present situation of delicate international balance, all these considerations should weigh heavily. Such is certainly no time to be applying the goad to those who are responsible for making fateful decisions. We need no men in public office who are little enough to play politics with war!

Futility in Fact

The terrific price of modern wars might be justified if they really accomplished anything of significant and permanent value. One historian dares to state that "The most unfortunate thing about war is that it accomplished nothing . . . all its sacrifices are vain . . . war does not settle anything." Most of us probably feel that he goes too far when he says that war does not settle anything.

We must admit, however, that he has a point if he is referring exclusively to modern wars. It does seem that war settled some issues at other times in history. We think of our own Revolution and the War Between the States as cases in point. It must be admitted, however, that modern wars seem to settle little if anything with finality. The victors are also the victims. No nation really seems to win. One gets the distinct impression that everybody really loses in the long run.

What Does War Cost?

On Christmas night in 1917, an incredible thing happened in a battle between an American regiment and the German counterpart. Fighting suddenly stopped and men leapt out of the trenches. The German soldiers ran toward the American lines while our men moved in the direction of the German entrenchments. They met in the No-Man's-Land in between. There they fraternized, exchanged cigarettes and chocolates, and sang Christmas carols together!

What Might Have Been . . .

Letters and substantiating affidavits have been submitted by men who actually took part in this incident. They were eventually driven back to their trenches by high command officers and told to get on with the war! However, some of them did so with a sudden disenchantment—and a haunting, nagging discontent. Later they pondered and discussed "what might have been." In retrospect, the suspicion persists that World War I might have ended during that first Christmas if it had been left to the men who were doing the fighting!

This incident is admittedly a singular one. And its implications are easily overdrawn. The issues were never that simple— nor the solution so easy. On the other hand is evidence abundant that sinister factors have frequently lengthened a war which should have been concluded quickly and neatly.

The Economic Truth

If we are to tell the truth about war we are forced to include a sad and sordid story about the manufacture of munitions and other war materials. It is a documented fact that some munitions makers have been international racketeers. They have been properly called "merchants of death" because it is their business to sell death—to increase the production of death. Highly paid lobbyists and powerfully organized influence peddlers are dedicated to the objective of shortening every period of peace and lengthening every period of war! Some munitions makers get rich on their high-profit military contracts while the nation's sons move dejected and disillusioned from one battlefield to the next. And the Congress increases taxes.

President Franklin D. Roosevelt never said a truer thing than when he said, "War is due in no small measure to the uncontrolled activities of the manufacturers and merchants of destruction, and it must be met by the concerted action of the peoples of all nations." The economic stake in war is tremendous. War pays big financial dividends!

Take a munitions company for example. Their's was indeed a significant part in the production for World War I. They even boasted that their powder won the war! If their powder brought peace, it also brought them plenty of profits! In the four years prior to World War I, their profits were only $6,000,000 a year. In the four years of the war they had an increase of 950%, or $58,000,000 per year profit. Steel companies did about as well. And other manufacturers came in for theirs.

The profits of a certain leather company jumped from $3,000,000 yearly to $15,000,000, and those of another company, from $4,000,000 to $73,000,000—an increase of 1,700%!

The leather producers sold Uncle Sam 35,000,000 pairs of hob-nailed shoes for that conflict—eight pairs to a soldier.

When the war was over we had 25,000,000 pairs left. Somebody produced a fantastic amount of mosquito netting and sold the military 20,000,000 nets, not one of which ever got to France. General Smedley Butler very facetiously remarked that if the war had lasted just a little bit longer those enterprising mosquito netting manufacturers would have sold Uncle Sam a couple of consignments of mosquitoes to plant in France so that more mosquito netting would be in order!

The airplane companies sold the government one billion dollars worth of airplanes for World War I, not one of which ever got into a battle in France. Most of them never left the ground. Moreover, we paid three billion for ships. Nearly one billion worth were of faulty construction and wouldn't float. The seams opened up and down they went to the bottom of the sea. But some shipbuilders became millionaires just the same.

Twenty-one thousand men admitted to becoming millionaires or better out of the profits made in that war. Of the 52 billion spent, 16 billion was considered profits for the manufacturers. That's how they got their wealth. But the G.I. Joes did the fighting. They went hungry in rat-infested dugouts, slept in the mud through cold and rain, spent sleepless nights ducking shells and shrapnel, dodged the bayonet thrust of the enemy. Some survived this only to be shot down at last by bullets made and sold to the enemy by their own brothers in this land.

Similar facts are available concerning World War II, the Korean conflict, and the Vietnam engagement. One example will suffice. We were told during the fifties of a dangerous "bomber gap," and intensive efforts were made to correct the situation. Among the planes which we kept on making in an effort to fill this "gap" was the B36. Hundreds of these planes are still sitting around at various places in the world. It is reported that pilots never wanted to fly them because not many pilots wanted to trust their lives in them. They were never considered to be good planes, but we kept on making them!

Finally, it was determined that there never was a bomber gap after all. We had spent six billion dollars on bombers and finally assembled nearly fifteen hundred of them. Only then did we discover that Russia never had more than 160 long range bombers at any one time. We spent billions in frenzied fear only to learn later that most of the Russian planes couldn't cross the ocean and return. The news never got out, however, until the money had been spent. Now you can strike up a good conversation with many Air Force officers on the subject. They will grin and admit, "Yeah, that was something, wasn't it? They never had over 150 after all."

It Costs to Kill

It has been estimated that in Caesar's day the cost of killing a man in battle was seventy-five cents. In Napoleon's time, the cost had increased to $3,000; by the time of the Civil War, it had reached $5,000; by the end of World War I, it rose to $21,000, and in World War II, the United States paid the equivalent of $50,000 per capita for its dead enemies. It is estimated that today it is costing the United States a quarter of a million dollars to kill each Viet Cong.

What have our wars cost us?

According to the Defense Department, World War I cost the United States $25,000,000,000. World War II cost $323,000,000,000. The Korean conflict totaled $20,000,-000,000 and in mid-1968, the war in Vietnam was costing approximately $30,000,000,000 per year! More than sixty percent of our total national budget is now allocated for defense and military purposes.

We need to face up to the economic truth about war. If there were some way to compute the total time, energy, and manpower invested in the military operations and wartime involvements of our young nation, it would amount to a fantastically staggering sum! It has been estimated that over half of the all-time collections for Internal Revenue in our country have been spent for the purposes of war!

If the nutritive value of a person's food during his growing years were so directed as to make his arm grow at the expense of his body—he would become a monster instead of a man! Some nations in history have, for that very reason, become monsters rather than men. It is indeed the concern of some of our most responsible citizens lest such deformity establish itself upon our own national image and function.

The material aspects of the cost of war are insignificant in comparison with the devastating moral and spiritual toll. The experience of war invariably deposits over the whole body of society a bitter film of hate which enters the pores and penetrates the central nervous system. The whole thought of life seems to be consumed in the vortex of hatred and revenge.

Suffering and Heartbreak

Several years ago a careful examination was made of the textbooks used in the public schools in a certain section of our country. It was discovered that some of them devoted as much as eighty percent—eighty pages out of every hundred of our history—describing wars and battles. In a reaction of disgust, somebody attempted the following analogy: Would you write the biography of a person by describing with eighty pages out of every hundred a pimple on his face? Then as an afterthought he admitted that the "pimple" was a poor illustration. War is really cancer—a social cancer!

No matter how nobly conceived or how cautiously executed, war cannot possibly be confined to the soldiers in battle. Villages are ravaged. The aged and infirm are overrun. Women and children suffer agony, deprivation, and death.

Back in the thirteenth century the city of Beziers in southern France was surrounded by the French Army. They had come in the name of God to hunt heretics. They began their search, and in less than six hours (one historian says five and a half!) they slaughtered every man, woman, and child in the city of twenty thousand people! The white crosses of Christ etched upon their tunics were drenched with the blood of their victims. The incident triggered one of the blackest periods of human history and lends itself to several obvious applications. It illustrates most dramatically the tendency of war to breed all kinds of savagery and barbarity.

Who *are* the real sufferers?

It is the innocents who suffer most in modern warfare. How much they really suffer is something we can only try to imagine. Yet we must, in conscience, really try. We must not dodge any facts. The Korean War left over four million refugees in bombed out circumstances. More than twice that number of refugees has already resulted from the Vietnam conflict.

We need to tell the truth about these horrors of war. Follow the advancing army and observe the writhing, tortured bodies of the injured. See the medics and their helicopter crews evacuate their mutilated buddies. Hear the ravings of those who have been knocked senseless and the cries of those who want to die and cannot. Walk up and down the corridors of the Walter Reed Hospital and behold the horror of war. Ponder then the horrifying and unspeakable atrocities which we inflict upon our enemies. Think and weep about the little children, the old men, the sobbing women—blasted to pieces by the bombs and scorched with napalm.

Most Americans Far Removed

Most Americans are so far removed from the actual engagement of recent wars that it is impossible for us to sense their full impact. To be sure, many families have lost men on foreign battle fields; and others have returned home with wounds that left them greatly handicapped for future usefulness and happiness. Yet the great majority of Americans have suffered no great inconveniences from the wars in which our nation has been engaged over the last hundred years.

Sure, we complain about the tax structure; but even then we are so much better off economically than most of the rest of the world that comparison is impossible! Admittedly there have been times when we did not have as much butter or bacon as we desired. There were years when gasoline was rationed and we were forced to postpone the pleasure trips which we espoused. We were short on sugar for a while, but we learned to drink coffee and tea without it. And some of our major industries had to be temporarily converted to manufacture implements of war instead of automobiles and washing machines! Yet life in America has only scarcely been touched by the horror of war.

The Real Suffering

It might do us good if we could live for a while in lands that have been ravaged by bombs and bloodshed. A visitor in Germany, following World War II, saw people living in cellars and basements of homes that had been totally wrecked by bombs. Many of the living quarters were damp and wet with mold and mildew. They were hardly fit for rats—much less human beings.

The occupants, existing on starvation rations, fell victim to tuberculosis by the tens of thousands. Walking amid the debris and diseased humanity gave one the feeling that he was walking within the walls of a charnel house! Standing in the midst of a prominent intersection in the heart of Berlin, one could look in any direction and see only stark ruin and bleak desolation. Not a building stood in its former state—the streets were still littered with the wreckage of falling roofs and walls.

Years later, the writer was similarly depressed by a visit to Poland. The great, proud city of Warsaw had been 85% demolished! The Jewish ghetto, comprising hundreds of thousands of women, children, and helpless men, was completely obliterated. The enemy swept through the densely populated area with explosives and flame throwers, reducing the entire section to a carnage of smoke and death.

In Prague, Czechoslovakia, the walls of one synagogue contain the names of 38,000 Jews—all slaughtered in the hatred and holocaust of war! One cannot help but be moved with alternating currents of admiration and revulsion as he scans these walls and reflects upon their sad significance.

And don't forget Korea! Recall the pictures and pathos reported among the repatriated prisoners of Freedom Village. Those who ministered to the wounded in army hospitals in Tokyo can tell you of the probing pain and the shattering emotions they felt. Witness now the carnage in Vietnam, depicted so movingly by pictures and reports. Cartoonist Herblock of the *Washington Post* identified compassionately with the helpless and frustrated civilian population. With deft and probing artistry, he depicted the rain of death and fire on the ground while airplanes cavorted in dogfights up above. The caption read: "I don't know if either side is winning, but I know who's losing."

War Is Madness

There were 66,000,000 casualties in World War II. Today we have at our finger tips the techniques of destruction that make the most frightening weapons of twenty years ago sound like toys. And still the nations taunt one another, tease one another, and threaten one another into absolute annihilation. We escalate an Asian civil war into what could become the end of the world.

This entire business of international relations would be an amusing little game—if it were not so thoroughly irrational! Reflect for a moment upon the crazy-quilt pattern which represents our American record in international relations:

In 1755 we became involved in the French and Indian War. We were told to hate the French and love the British.

In 1776 we achieved an American Revolution. We were told to hate the British and love the French.

In 1799 we fought our sea battles with the French and were told to hate the French again.

In 1812 we fought again—and were told to hate the British and love the French.

In 1846 we got involved in the Mexican War. We hated the Mexicans and loved one another.

In 1861 we launched the Civil War; the North was told to hate the South, and the South was told to hate the North.

In 1898 we fought the Spanish-American War. We were told to hate the Spaniards. Today Spain is a Fascist dictatorship, and we are advised that she is our friend.

In 1900 came the Boxer Rebellion. We were told to hate the Chinese. In 1937 Japan invaded China, and we were told to hate the Japanese and begin to love the Chinese. Today the tables are turned, and we love Japan and hate China—except for that part of China that endures on an off-shore island.

In 1915 the Italians joined the Allies in the first World War. We loved them. In 1935 they invaded Ethiopia and we hated them.

In 1939 Russia invaded Finland. We hated Russia and loved Finland. In 1941 Russia was fighting with us, Finland with the Nazis. We hated the Fins and loved the Russians. Today Russia is anathema.

In Korea we hated everyone north of an imaginary line and loved everyone south of the same line. Now in Vietnam, we are even more confused, with lines refusing to stay drawn and with indiscriminate bombardments spreading the hate across the countryside.

So it has been and so it continues—in season and out of season. Men have been taught to hate and to destroy.

Again and again human flesh rots in the soil of the earth—and to what purpose?

Waste of muscle, waste of brain;
Waste of patience, waste of pain;
Waste of manhood, waste of health;
Waste of beauty, waste of wealth;
Waste of blood and waste of tears;
Waste of youth's most precious years;
Waste of ways the saints have trod;
Waste of glory, waste of God—War!

War Is Evil

Cordell Hull said, "War is not an act of God; it is a crime of man." All wars are civil wars in the sight of God. They are one son hating and killing another son—one brother pitted against another brother.

It is easy for a nation of people to slip gradually into a war psychosis. Such is a bona fide mental illness, a hysteria born of hatred and fear. We need to remind ourselves of this. We must assume responsibility for telling the world that war is a hypocrite, a cheat, and a liar! War prates about "the preservation of our way of life" and then requires for its pursuit a modification of that way of life which leads to regimentations and controls which we never seem to be able to wholly cast off when war is over!

C. J. Cadoux is convinced that there is a "chronic tendency toward war to beget more war." And Emil Brunner reminds us that "we never see the real meaning of 'original sin,' we never perceive the depth and universality of evil, or what evil really means in the depths, until we are obliged to be something which, in itself, is evil." He is saying that we do not personally experience the inner torture of sin and evil until we are involved by identity and association with something which in an isolated situation would be revolting and unthinkable!

World War II taught us what we did not want to believe— that man was still capable of behaving very, very badly! We wrote a new chapter on man's inhumanity to man! Many people had begun to believe that progress was inevitable—that all man needed was money, food, and freedom in order to rise step-by-step to his very highest pinnacle.

We had permitted ourselves to believe that utopia would certainly arrive if everybody could get a good job and a good home. If we would only pursue the good neighbor policy and treat every man as a blood-born brother, we should regain our paradise! Sin became something outmoded or reserved merely for the pulpit. Modern men and women, we reasoned, need not worry about their own sins or the sins of the world. It would eventually be a good world. It just had to be—with all the modern inventions, the leisure time, and the inevitable progress which would prevail.

Then, all of a sudden, our little bubble burst! Our idealistic image of humanity fell like Lucifer's fall from heaven. We saw and heard about atrocities unspeakable to relate and too terrible to believe. Only after the war was over and some of our people were commissioned to go and see with their own eyes, did we begin to believe that the things reported really happened. Death chambers, torture camps, human incinerators—this is what war had done. War had taught man to hate. War had communicated to millions the futility of life. War had given a new meaning to the word "annihilism." War made our blood boil in one moment and freeze in our veins the next. Of course the war criminals have now been tried, convicted, and put to death; but what success have we had in efforts at rehabilitation of the people they trained and taught to think and act as beasts? What a revelation war becomes as to the possibilities of baseness in human nature!

The tendencies to war lie deep within the soul of every man. We may not be able to see any clear nexus of cause and effect in a process sure to bring about a war, but it is there. The dynamics are similar in character to those, which in other men, have directly precipitated great tragedy. In their own way, we must admit that they have caused distress and hurt to people around us. There is sin in every life.

When we are able to hold ourselves guiltless in respect to any particular war, we have to admit that this blamelessness results from God's grace alone. Had we been in a position of greater power (therefore of greater temptation) we might well have fallen as low as the criminal dictators who must bear the primary guilt in the aforementioned circumstances. The worst we can say of war is that it is the outcome of sin. Any efforts to "outlaw war" are nonsensical unless we first agree to outlaw sin! Where sin is, sooner or later war will inevitably manifest itself in one or another of its many forms.

We must understand then that war is the type and embodiment of all human sin—that black ingratitude and degradation which leads men to spurn the call of God. It is that dark tendency and terror of our natures which leads us to trample our ideals under foot, violate the rights of others, and give in to our own lusts and cravings.

God Suffers Too

Our hearts bleed for all those victims of war who have been maimed and broken. We are touched to the depths by those who are gripped in slavery and starvation, who have lost their homes, their loved ones and the liberty of life itself. We search our souls and feel in the depths an agony unspeakable and unatoned.

But God sees it, too! He also feels the pain and the anguish. In human sin he sees the utter corruption of all that is highest in his great universe. The Master Architect is left with his most glorious building in ruins. The Great Creator mourns over his broken creation. The captain and leader of God's hosts is faced by the mutiny and desertion of the followers to whom he has given his very best.

No matter how sensitive we may be, we cannot begin to feel the depths of pain our Lord feels when he beholds the holocaust of war. When we look upon the horror and havoc of the battlefields of the nations, we should be reminded of the prophets reverent attempt to place the assessment on the lips of the Divine Sufferer himself: "Behold, and see if there be any sorrow like unto my sorrow" (Lamentations 1:12, KJV).

A little girl heard her minister tell of the suffering of the people of the earth in the war areas. She was very disturbed about the visions and impressions which these scenes etched upon her tender soul. At bedtime she was still upset and sobbed herself to sleep. Next morning she lifted her tear-stained face to her mother and said, "God must have cried himself to sleep last night."

Such is the truth about war. It hurts and maims. It cuts and kills. It brings suffering unspeakable to man. But the Christian understands that it hurts God most of all.

Profile of a Pacifist

Some people refuse to participate in war of any kind. They are called *pacifists*. In the Latin Bible the word for peacemakers is *pacifici,* the direct English form of which is *pacifists*.

Some who preach or practice pacifism prefer the term nonresistance. They, too, refuse to participate in or lend support to any type of warfare. They renounce all coercion, even non-violent coercion. This philosophy is therefore primarily negative in its connotation.

But pacifism is a positive expression, and it covers many types of opposition to war. Some modern pacifists are opposed to all wars, and some are not. Some establish their position in what they believe to be the teachings of the Bible and the will of God. Others have reached a decision through logic and reason.

The committed pacifist concludes that there is nothing left to do but renounce all war. He is convinced that war encourages men to sin. He can catalogue his complaints, and the following outline summarizes his feelings about all war:

(1) He believes that it poisons the air with lies, that the first casualty is always truth. The result is "managed news" and slanted views. We call it propaganda. The design is to make the enemy look as bad as possible and stir up enthusiasm for the conflict.

(2) He is convinced that war breeds hate; therefore, the second casualty is always love. Here lies the basis of "man's

63

inhumanity to man." In war other people become less than
persons. They are no longer treated as human beings. They are
things—to be damaged or destroyed.

(3) He affirms that war makes men sin economically. War
breeds graft and greed. It makes crooks and racketeers. It lays
waste to the resources which could buy bread and education for
the dispossessed. Vietnam is a case in point: The lush green
valleys of an agrarian economy are being torn asunder by the
havoc of battle.

(4) He feels that it collapses man's character by dulling and
even killing the conscience! We become accustomed to violence.
Death is the order of the day. The call of the helpless and the
hopeless no longer moves us. We call it "compassion fatigue."

(5) He claims that war lays hold of the finest virtues and
prostitutes them. Patriotism, heroism, and idealism all suffer
from this abnormal scourge. It converts these wholesome characteristics into instruments of destruction.

(6) He believes that war negates the witness of Christ and
the church. The pacifist believes that the Christian hereby con-
tradicts himself. His interpretation of the Christian gospel concludes that if war is right, Christianity is wrong. He therefore
reasons that if Christianity is to prevail, then war must go!

Early Christianity

The early church condemned war. The great majority of
Christians refused participation in war—often at the cost of
death or severe punishment. Justin Martyr (A.D. 114) believed
the spirit of war and the spirit of Jesus Christ to be absolutely
irreconcilable. Tertullian (about A.D. 145) searched in vain for
a way to enable a Christian to bear arms and keep his conscience clear. Cyprian, of the third century, labeled war "whole-
sale murder."

Some early Christian sources indicate that from the middle of
the first century to the latter part of the second century no

Christian soldier is known to have existed. But Tertullian, for one, confirms the assumption that some believers did enter the military. He specifically indicates that there were Christians in the armed services at the turn of the second century.

He wrote about a Christian soldier who refused to wear a garland on the emperor's birthday, a courtesy of the subjects acknowledging the ruler's divinity. He cites this as one of the examples of "heathen collusion" and insists that violence and bloodshed are not consonant with the Christian way of life and the peace-making motif. We have records of several instances where Christians accepted death as punishment with the simple resignation, "I am a Christian, and therefore I cannot fight."

The church continued to be consistently pacifist until the emperor Constantine declared Christianity to be the official religion of the Roman Empire in the fourth century A.D. Because of this alliance the church became a participant of war— sometimes a sponsor of war! It gave its blessing to various "wars" and literally precipitated military conflict. It became involved in civil and social responsibilities.

The preservation of law and order, along with the repression of anarchy, became increasingly incumbent. There are indeed dark centuries in history where the church appears to be carrying the cross of Jesus in one hand and a dripping sword in the other!

It is a fact, however, that the Roman Catholic Church attempted to maintain the pacifist attitude. It created monastic communities which practiced the way of love and peace. Members of the clergy were required to vow complete abstention from any war-like activities. There were some admitted defections from this ideal, however, and some semi-monastic orders began openly to bear arms.

The pacifist philosophy persisted through the centuries, emerging from time to time as a powerful and persuasive deterrent to violence and bloodshed. The Waldenses' championed its resurgence in the Middle Ages. Other sects of dissenters and "free church" movements shed blood and paid dearly in support of the pacifist cause.

Anabaptists emerged in the fifteenth and sixteenth centuries as one of the identifiable sects who consistently refused to bear arms and who advocated complete separation from a sinful social order. The Mennonites steadily rejected military service and exemplified the philosophy of nonresistance. Both of these groups have survived.

The Mennonites gradually modified their position in respect to the social order in general, and especially social and medical services in time of war. The modern Baptists, however, reflect more of the influence of the English Puritans than of their Anabaptist forefathers, and have never officially established any pacifist posture.

Pacifists in History

Since the Reformation the most credit for pacifistic leadership must go to the Mennonites. They receive great support and encouragement from many other individuals and groups who likewise have had a share in maintaining the doctrine and practice of pacifism.

Outstanding and vocal assistance has come from the Society of Friends (Quakers). From its earliest stages this group has maintained a persistent position against war. The Church of the Brethren, founded in 1708, has subscribed tenaciously to the biblical doctrine of nonresistance.

William Penn exemplified the Quaker commitment in his dealings with the American Indians. Quakers have maintained consistently their conscientious objection to war, and at the same time, they have demonstrated an intense social concern. In time of war, their ambulance units have symbolized the spirit of the Quakers to share in social and national involvement wherever possible without violation of their religious convictions.

In 1815, David Low Dodge, a Presbyterian layman, established the New York Peace Society. He was a devout student and practitioner of the biblical teachings on nonresistance.

A few years later, Adain Ballou emerged as another advocate of nonresistance. His doctrine was not as biblically oriented as that of Dodge. He was deeply committed, however, and very vocal on the subject of his beliefs.

Both of these men avoided political activity because they were convinced that such would compromise their position and be inconsistent with the philosophy of nonresistance.

These men and others maintained the promotion of peace in an organized way. They published literature, spoke at public forums, delivered sermons in pulpits, and pursued their objective in every conceivable manner. A number of people shared their views, and although the number was never large, their activity was great.

They launched a significant campaign which eventually came to be known as "the peace movement" of the early nineteenth century. So zealous were the adherents and so promising its creed that the peace movement has become a permanent institution in American life. Records indicate that it has always declined somewhat in times of war; but with each cessation of international hostility it has usually become more active than before.

Modern Pacifists

The modern pacifist agrees with his predecessor that war is a massive evil, man's chief collective sin. He believes that it destroys the best in human life and arouses the worst in men. Some therefore believe that any kind of peace is better than war! They contend that war accomplishes no good result. They feel that violence tends to breed violence. They look upon nuclear war as absolute insanity. Stockpiling nuclear weapons is to act like a madman!

On the other hand many modern pacifists agree to participate in military service in times of national crisis!

But they propose a program of education for peace—and insist that if it is done zealously and effectively, war itself will eventually be abolished. They believe that if statesmen can be educated to see that peace is better than war they will find ways to avoid waging war. They believe that if the church and press do their duty within a reasonable number of years the scourge of war can be completely wiped out of human society.

Much of their reasoning is drawn from the New Testament. More of it, however, stems from eighteenth century philosophers of France and England who believed in the inevitable progress of man. They make the mistake of emphasizing the dignity and goodness of man, along with his unlimited potentialities—to the neglect of the ultimate power of sin. They tend to be too optimistic regarding the possibilities for social progress and the achievements of human intelligence. Such a view makes Christ the example rather than the Redeemer of mankind and ignores the need for personal regeneration. Step-by-step it has led to modern religious liberalism and the popular idealistic pacifism of the twentieth century.

Gandhi of India championed the idea of nonviolent resistance. He was influenced, to some extent, by Tolstoy. But the teachings of Jesus also made a great impression upon him. His own Hindu religion emphasized the idea of sacrificial suffering. Gandhi applied this concept of victorious suffering to political relationships as a means of appeasing human tyrants. He engaged in fasting and other forms of suffering in an effort to make his point. He refused to pay taxes and engaged in deliberate efforts to embarrass his British rulers. He resorted to numerous techniques but never employed violence.

This is nonviolent resistance—not to be confused with simple nonresistance or peace. It was a new form of warfare! For nonviolent resistance is still resistance. It is a form of coercion or compulsion. Its purpose is to compel the other side to capitulate.

Some insist that there is a sharp distinction between nonviolence and New Testament nonresistance. They insist that the doctrine of the New Testament is an absolute nonresistance which makes no compromise with situational politics. They resent efforts to make a militarist out of Jesus by arguing that he drove the men out of the temple. They observe also that pacifists engage in an equally futile attempt to accommodate the nonresistance of Jesus to their own nonviolent concepts. It has even been suggested that Christ ended his life on the cross because he had not completely mastered the technique of nonviolence. According to this argument he must be regarded as a guide who is inferior to Gandhi, but who must be given credit for initiating the movement which produces men like Gandhi.

Christian pacifists generally fall within two distinct categories: legalistic and redemptive. A literal rendering of such passages as Ex. 20:13; Matt. 5:39; and Matt. 26:52 provides a foundation for the legalistic position. They are not concerned about the "witness" they bear because they do not expect to influence any significant segment of the unregenerate. Of little consideration is the social consequence of their actions. Some of our most zealous small denominations support this view, confident that Christians will always be "sheep among wolves."

The position of the redemptive pacifist is more dynamic. He believes that just as Jesus' sufferings were redemptive, nonviolent resistance to tyranny will ultimately prove similarly effective. The example of Christ and the early church are held up as normative standards regarding participation in war. The New Testament concept of love is presented as the basis of redemptive pacifism. This becomes the ethical imperative for the Christian because it reflects the essential nature of his Christ. This involves more than goodwill or kindness; it is giving without request or expectation of reward. It is all inclusive (Matt.

5:38f) and uncalculating (Matt. 5:10). Christian men and women are to recompense no man "evil for evil." They argue that retribution and vengeance belong to God; therefore war is out of the question.

The redemptive pacifist literally believes and practices the principle of overcoming evil with good. The counsel of the apostle Paul is taken to heart: "If your enemy is hungry, feed him; if he is thirsty, give him drink; for by so doing you will heap burning coals upon his head." (Rom. 12:20–21). It must be admitted that when Jesus was being crucified he did not attempt to retaliate. He, therefore, became an example for the redemptive pacifist. While on the cross he prayed to the Father to forgive those who were putting him to death. They infer that Jesus deliberately lost the battle in order to win men, while war crushes men in order to win the battle.

The Uncompromising Pacifist

An anonymous diary of Civil War days raised the following question: "Is it possible that there can be truth in the old notion that, in times of great national trial and excitement, so many men go mad . . . that madness becomes a sort of epidemic?" The modern pacifist believes strongly that the answer is in the affirmative. In fact, he believes it so strongly that his own excited proclamation of this probability becomes a sort of epidemic of madness within itself.

The hardcore pacifist of our time is fairly represented by the following typical affirmations.

"We cannot accept or endorse war as a Christian means of settling a dispute or pursuing a policy, however good that policy may be."

"We cannot sanction or support a preventive war—that is, an attack launched against an enemy before he strikes, hoping thereby to cripple his blow and save ourselves wide scale destruction."

"We cannot endorse or acquiesce in either the enslavement of or domination of the world or any part of it by any one power—whether Russia or the United States." (This is why many religious pronouncements have rejected our nation's foreign policy. They believe that our main purpose has been to build strong allies rather than to build strong peoples.)

"We cannot accept or endorse the policy of massive retaliation as being in any sense an expression of the Christian commitment. It is, in fact, a negation of the fundamental purpose of the gospel which is summed up in the word reconciliation."

For these reasons many of the large and powerful church bodies in the United States have taken a firm stand against universal military training. Resolutions have been passed, appeals have been made to the President and to Congress, and unqualified opposition has been registered.

(1) They believe that a wholesome Christian character can best be developed in a context of normal social relationships, and they are convinced that to place young men in the decidedly abnormal atmosphere of training camps for any period of time is morally degrading.

(2) They believe in freedom and democracy as valid ideals for America and are convinced that the enactment of universal military training tends to jeopardize both.

(3) They believe in the possibility of world peace, and are convinced that universal military training as an official position in the United States will endanger the achievement of this objective.

Several years ago Harry Emerson Fosdick preached an impassioned sermon titled "The Unknown Soldier." Considered by many as the most influential preacher in America, he rallied considerable response with these words:

"I renounce war. I renounce war because of what it does to our own men. I renounce war because of what it compels us to do to our enemies. I renounce war for its consequences, for the

lies it lives on and propagates, for the undying hatreds it
arouses, for the starvation that stalks after it. I renounce war
and never again, directly or indirectly, will I sanction or support
another! O Unknown Soldier, in penitent reparation I make you
that pledge."

We are seeing a resurgence of pacifism among clergymen.
Thousands of ministers and priests are joining in protest movements against the war in Vietnam. They are preaching sermons,
writing books, and submitting magazine articles in expression of
their unqualified opposition to war.

Conscientious Objectors

The conscientious objector may be a person who conscientiously objects to serving in any war under any circumstances;
on the other hand, he may be a person who objects to participation in a definite phase of a specific war!

To take upon one's conscience the responsibility for choosing
a particular conflict in which to participate is indeed a big order.
It requires an objective and comprehensive look at all the issues
involved. Such a person sees himself as excusable on conscience
for a group of reasons such as the following:

(1) He believes that he has made a serious examination of
the issues of the particular war in question and conscientiously
declines to participate; (2) He believes sincerely that he is
capable of responsible, moral reasoning in an attempt to relate
his convictions to the data at hand; (3) He is dedicated to an
effort to give "political expression" to his convictions; (4) He is
willing to participate in a military role of a different nature; (5)
He is willing to accept whatever penalties and punishments may
be imposed upon him because of his stand.

Ideally, Christians are neither revolutionaries nor reactionar-
ies. They will have no part with anarchy. Their religion will not
allow them to be disloyal citizens of their own country. The
New Testament, however, seems clearly to teach that a Chris-

tian may disobey his state, if and when the state orders him to sin. This, of course, is open to interpretation. If a person arrives at the conviction that his government has ordered him to do that which in his conscience violates the law of God, then the example of Simon Peter becomes his guide: "We must obey God rather than man." (Acts 5:29).

In our society this principle is recognized by both the state and the church. In recent years the church has repeated its position that, when a man feels in his conscience that he would have to sin to obey the State, he has the right and the privilege to disobey.

America has recognized this right by allowing conscientious objection to war. If a Christian feels that he cannot take up arms because it violates his religious convictions, he may register as a "conscientious objector." Under these conditions he will not be compelled to carry arms but will be permitted to serve in a noncombat assignment. This exception is denied, of course, by non-Christian nations. It is because America was founded on Christian principles that this consideration of the conscientious objector has been maintained as a part of our democratic heritage.

It must be emphasized that when a pacifist conscientiously follows what he considers to be the example of Christ, he must not be branded a lowly coward! It may be that he demonstrates remarkable personal courage. He dedicates his radical nonresistance toward a constructive and powerful Christian witness.

Many conscientious objectors feel only that they must stop short of taking a human life. They will risk their lives in the medical corps, serve in mechanical or clerical positions, work in plants, buy bonds, pay taxes and support the war effort in many other ways. All the while, however, they suffer deeply in that such involvement identifies them with the sin of their nation.

We all need to be reminded of the example of our honored ancestors. Had they not valued liberty and honor more than life itself, America would not be here today—a bulwark of hope and confidence in an unstable world. There is evidence that many of them resorted only reluctantly to the use of cannon and bayonet. They would have much preferred the "quiet life" to their muskets and the military.

Succeeding generations have always found strength and inspiration in their determination to defend the right at any cost. Once an unwillingness to stand for those things has been expressed, a potential menace becomes an overwhelming probability. One cannot avoid the suspicion that with a continuing expansion of the philosophy of nonresistance all vestiges of freedom will soon disappear from all the earth!

Was Jesus a Pacifist?

It is difficult to reconcile an act of war with the prevailing spirit of the Master. War attempts to overcome evil by inflicting injury. Jesus recommended the enduring of injury. War tends to look upon men as "things" while Jesus always treated them as persons made in the image of God and capable of responding to his redemptive love. War is dedicated to crippling or killing the enemy. Jesus preferred to kill the enmity! War is geared to crush men in order to achieve victory. Jesus was willing to be crushed in order to win men.

Jesus taught and practiced the principle of "agape" love. He proposed nonresistance and nonretaliation (Matt. 5). Love for God and man represented the essence and summary of his teachings concerning man's moral and ethical obligations. This law of love was inclusive of the good and the bad, the friend and the foe. Pacifist interpreters find it inconceivable that love for the enemy is fulfilled by killing him in war.

The life of Jesus provides a strong and eloquent example for the Christian pacifist position. He showed great restraint in the presence of enemies and persecutors. The cross, itself, demonstrates the philosophy of Jesus in dealing with injustice and force. It marks the climax of his teaching and preaching of peace and goodwill to men. He prayed for his enemies and accepted the infinite suffering of the cross in order to bring redemption to mankind.

On the other hand we cannot conceive of his absolute noninterference in case of threatened mutilation or barbarity upon other persons. If a drunk fiend were to enter a home, strangle a man's child, and grab his wife by the throat, we cannot believe that Jesus would simply pray for him!

Our Lord used his divine power to thwart his enemies who would have thrown him from the execution bluff in Nazareth. There is no record in this instance that he first tried a program of nonresistance and prayer! He stunned them with the power of his eyes and he seared them with righteous indignation. He declared that he had not come to bring peace but war; and all the hermeneutical hair-splitting of the ages will not change the opinion of many that he was speaking of actual human warfare.

So we have a confusing picture. In the historical Jesus we have examples of both positions. His command to Peter illustrates our problem: "Put up again thy sword into his place: for all they that take the sword shall perish with the sword." (Matt. 26:52, KJV).

Are we justified in drawing the conclusion from this one verse that Jesus taught that war is never, under any circumstances, to be tolerated? A careful reading of the entire passage convinces many serious students that Jesus approved the use of the sword —if not for offense, then at least for defense. He certainly showed his belief that some objectives are worth dying for. He could not be identified with the group we have today who say so glibly (and almost irrelevantly!), "Better Red than dead."

The Christ of the Bible does not fall into the pattern of a hard-core pacifist. The Bible is not a pacifist book. It doesn't condone saber-rattling for selfish purposes—either on the part of individuals or government. Nor does it recommend that we look on resignedly while nations are being devastated. It never suggests that strong men stand by while their wives are being violated and their children murdered before their very eyes! The Bible is a realistic book and the image of the Christ is the image of a responsible and sensitive realist.

A Christian Critique

The pacifist says war is the worst of all evils, while the nonpacifist says there are worse things than war. It is at best a choice between relative evils. This is the tragic dilemma of Christian living at its sharpest.

Roland H. Bainton warns against the pitfall of irresponsible irrelevance in *Christian Attitudes Toward War and Peace.* He explains that the typical pacifist is motivated by a concern to appear before God with clean hands and a pure heart. He refuses to become involved for fear he will become contaminated. But Dr. Bainton, who identifies himself as a pacifist, observes that detachment means irrelevance and again confronts the Christian with a dilemma. No matter how worthy the motive, irrelevance is indefensible. Justice requires involvement. Involvement demands action. The choices which confront the pacifist are grim indeed.

During a youth conference a question was turned in which asks whether a nonpacifist can be a Christian at all! Such an insinuation would have been considered an impertinence except for the wonderful spirit of openness and honest inquiry which prevailed. The question immediately calls to mind the tens of thousands of brave Christian men and women who have laid down their lives for their liberty. It reminds us of the thousands of chaplains in the Army, Navy and Air Force. Were they hypocrites? Or did they do the only thing which honor and integrity dictated?

It all raises a question as to where our vaunted ideals and our national honor might be at this time had it not been for such dedicated and unselfish patriots. It is permissible to assume that we might now be under the power of some foreign foe and/or political ideology.

What would become of the pacifists if there were not some sturdy nonpacifists around to intercede in their behalf? Suppose, for example, that one takes the complete pacifist view: Great—he lives a life of comparative safety. That safety depends, however, upon sacrifice of other men whom he accuses of taking less than a Christian attitude. But their compassionate efforts to protect his home, provide food and care for his wife and children are not seen as "Christian" acts!

The pacifist position is untenable. It is inconsistent and intolerable. Some of its critics use the word *irrational*. After all, some form of coercive action is necessary to guarantee social order and stability. A government must attempt to protect its people from aggression.

Nevertheless the pacifists are committed to the dream of a day when swords will be beaten into plowshares. They will keep right on opposing every effort to beat the plowshares into swords.

A Christian Rationale

"A man who has nothing which he cares about more than his personal safety is a miserable creature who has no chance of being free—unless made and kept so by the exertions of better men than himself."

In these words John Stuart Mill established an image and presented a challenge for these "better men." With equal insight he added: "War is an ugly thing, but not the ugliest of things: the decayed and degraded state of moral and patriotic feeling which thinks nothing worth a war—is worse."

Let's face it: Physical force is indispensable. We are nowhere near a time when governments can exist without armed force. This is true and will continue to be true as long as there are men and groups so retarded that they have no other resource by which to make their point. Or they do not have the ingenuity to employ it. Such families, cities, and nations are impoverished in social and moral strength and must fall back on something. So they resort to violence.

Those who are threatened by such onslaughts find themselves confronted with retaliation in king—or anarchy! The less there is of such conflict, in any nation or on any part of the globe, the further removed we are from barbarism, and the nearer we approach the ideal of Christian civilization.

But the time is not yet!

Police Protection

The ideal of Christianity is final and universal peace, and it is the duty of nations to dispense with physical force as fast and as far as possible. But it cannot be done suddenly—disbanding all armies and police organizations—leaving the world to think that there is no government! To do so would expose the human family to fatal brutalities, make the tyrant more tyrannical, and the lawless more lawless. Until society is stronger in the social, intellectual, and moral elements, we must reluctantly employ the instrument of force.

The use of armed strength, as such, is neither morally right nor morally wrong. It is the uses to which it is put—the times, the places, the amount, and the purposes—which determine the moral or immoral use of force. At our particular stage of the development of mankind, failure to use such force in the proper time and place and for the proper purposes could be indescribably disastrous and downright immoral.

Most of us share an absolute abhorrence of war, but the sacrifice of principle and the loss of freedom are worse than the loss of life. Both principle and freedom become involved in international conflict. We should make sure that our cause is just, then willingly pay the price.

We must have laws, courts, the police, and the armed forces to maintain peace and order in the land. We must have respect for law and order in our country. Otherwise, we would have bedlam and chaos. Evil must be restrained and evil-doers must be challenged for the good of all.

At the close of World War I the isolationist forces consolidated to prevent America's entrance into the League of Nations. The contention was that we must not agree to use force, not even economic force, to suppress war, so we stayed out. Since that day we have come to see the fallacy of that earlier position. We have repeatedly joined with other peace loving nations in the use of force to deter war-mad men and nations who would disturb the peace of the world.

We must guard against pressing the analogy too far, but it is something like what we do in the local community, in the state, and within the nation. When someone runs amuck, shoots up the town, commits murder or other disturbances, we use force and such punishment as fits the crime according to the law. In our urban centers we spend large amounts of money and employ professional personnel to administer and enforce the law. Otherwise, we would have no protection. Life and limb would be in danger. The state and nation would be at the mercy of violent and antisocial people.

This policy has provided us with an orderly process of protecting our society within the nation. Logic suggests that within our world society a similar process must be utilized in order that those who want peace may be saved from the ravages of war mania and the delusions of violent men.

In Defense of the Military

It is a mistake to look upon the military as no more than a fighting machine in the event of war and as a glorified police force in days of peace. Non-military people often reveal an alarming lack of understanding at this point. In the two decades following World War I, we went through a period of casual disdain and occasional hostility toward the Army and Navy of the United States.

And after World War II, it seemed for a time that the lines of an old English ballad, written nearly three centuries ago, would come true for us once again:

> "God and the soldier we adore,
> In times of danger, not before;
> The danger past, and all things righted,
> God is forgotten and the soldier slighted."

The writer has enjoyed close personal acquaintance with many "career" people in the respective military organizations. He has experienced a profound and growing appreciation for the people of this profession.

It is good for us to remember that, historically, the military served the frontier and established order in our young republic. The military institution will continue to stand between anarchy and order and to uphold our way of life in the face of enemy action.

The military profession has made a significant contribution toward all instruments of civilization, progress, and life-enrichment. These Americans have braved the heat of the tropics and the cold of the arctic in placing us in their debt! They have helped to dig canals, guard forest preserves, build mountain roads, and irrigate arid acres. Men of the military have made significant marks in such fields as exploration, transportation, medicine, engineering, atomic energy, and the space probe. They are dedicated to the enrichment and implementation of our social progress and our spiritual destiny.

On February 2, 1935, the steamer *Tung Chow* was attacked by pirates. From its base in Shanghai it was carrying English and American children back from the holidays to their boarding school at Crefoo. Suppose the captain had suddenly become pacifist and decided that it was wrong to resist and retaliate. We have only to permit our imaginations to run free for a moment to arrive at some terrifying probabilities. English and American girls in their teens would have been captured by these pirates and carried off to become prostitutes for years to come. But here is what really happened: The captain signaled for help and the pirate vessel was sunk before the children could be captured!

We need to be reminded that an aircraft carrier had to be in existence, fighter planes had to be manned, and a British destroyer had to be on duty before such a rescue mission could have been carried out. Some pacifists try to convince us that the very existence of such instruments is a crime against God. If to repel such an aggressor is considered wrong, then it must be less wrong than to permit innocent people to fall into the hands of unscrupulous maniacs!

There are those among us who insist that such actions only encourage war and will lead ultimately to a militarist state. It does not seem to necessarily follow that this would be the case. So long as a nation and its leaders are aware of the dangers of insidious militarism, proper and adequate steps can be made to avoid such a catstrophe.

At the same time, the alternatives demand analysis: As the lesser of two evils, it would be far better to succumb to a militarism of our own than to fall by default to the tyranny of a foreign despot! As matters now stand, there are those in the world who have vowed to "bury us!" If we lower our guard they are certain to infiltrate our ranks and overtake our society. They would despoil our women, brutalize our children, enslave our men, abolish all ownership of property and attempt to eliminate faith in God. That is the startling alternative!

Biblical Sanction

A preacher describes a modern New England worship service as "a very docile preacher trying to persuade an audience of docile men and women to 'please be just a little more docile.' " He makes a point of the fact that these are mistaken disciples of the Christ of God. The long-haired Jesus which they worship is only "half a Christ": It is just a caricature made to appear simply as sweetness and light personified! The followers are more likely disciples of Gandhi or Tolstoy than Jesus Christ.

We need to tear these spurious Christs from our minds and from our hearts! We need to remove them from our walls and from our minds—and "see the real Christ stand up"—in his moral majesty—against every force of evil throughout the world!

The majority of biblical scholars find great consistency between the ethics of Jesus Christ and the restraint of evil by force. To defend an individual or a nation, even at the risk of one's life, is considered to be in accordance with justice, intelligence, and responsibility. It is not incompatible with Christian love.

The heroes of our faith are men "who subdued kingdoms" and placed commitment to righteousness above life itself. It was of an army officer that our Lord said: "I have not found so great faith, no not in Israel." It was to the home of an army officer that God sent Peter to win the first fruits of the gospel in the Gentile world. On them the Holy Spirit came in his miraculous baptism, shown by the gift of tongues. The former of these military men was the first to believe "with all his house." The second of them did likewise. Jesus marveled at their faith and commended their character.

That the Scriptures should magnify such conversions of Jesus with soldiers before and after Pentecost without a hint that they are to give up the bearing of arms for their government, shows the utter absence of radical pacifism in mind or message.

The apostle Paul regarded "rulers and magistrates" as divinely ordained powers to maintain justice and thus to fulfil God's will for social order and equity. He declared that the powers of state are ordained of God, along with the authority to preserve order and prevent anarchy. This logic prevails on the local level and projects itself into an international application.

When leaders become irresponsible they are to be replaced. When this cannot be done by orderly means such as the democratic election process, it may have to be accomplished by violence in the public interest. This may sometimes involve the military vanquishment of a leader and his supporters. Hitler and

Napoleon are historic examples of this necessity. The means was justified in the interest of liberty and integrity.

A "Just" War

There have been some just wars in history. The Revolutionary War in America is justified because its purpose was to break the tyranny of the Crown and open the gates of freedom to the new republic. The War Between the States is justified in history by its sociological, theological, and economic implications—the emancipation of slaves. The war in Vietnam is justified in at least two respects: First, in its objective to help a helpless nation, and second, by its role in the containment of Communism.

It is to be admitted that one assumes a terrific responsibility when he labels any war a "just war." Nobody is ever completely in the right and none ever totally in the wrong. Sinful motives are always mixed up with good intentions. No idealistic vision of justice is pure, for man is sinful. And the procedures of warfare are always so degrading that the early idealism is likely to be lost. Unintended motivations emerge and vengeful policies so easily prevail.

Therefore, only reluctantly can a Christian participate. But when duty, justice, and honor demand it, he will! It is better to fight than to allow tyranny to flourish or for anarchy to deprive man of justice and opportunity.

Christians must see to it that the element of justice be kept in proper perspective however much it may be mixed with lower motives and distorted by sinful pretentions. We must demand that the outcome of such a war be infinitely better than the alternative.

If we take the position that there are no just wars, then we are forced to deny the right of our police to deter criminals. We need to understand that evil can get such control of men and nations that armed resistance becomes a necessity. There are

times when not to participate in violence is in itself to violate the
welfare of society itself.

> O gentlemen, the time of life is short!
> To spend that shortness basely were too long
> If life did ride upon a dial's point,
> Still ending at the arrival of an hour.
> And if we live, we live to tread on kings;
> If die, brave death, when princes die with us!
> Now, for our consciences, the arms are fair,
> When the intent of bearing them is just.
>
> *Henry IV*

Logic again dictates that a police force must be maintained
and that a military establishment must be provided. There are
not only lawless citizens but lawless states, which are bent on
disturbing the order of justice within human society and pursuing their own selfish designs at the expense of neighboring
persons, groups, or nations. Against these the state must take up
arms, sometimes in redress of grave injury and wrong. More
often, however, it is in defense of another's right to freedom and
self-determination. We must always be responsive to an unpro-
voked attack upon ourselves or those who share our fundamental commitments to life, liberty, and happiness.

This doctrine does not justify every war, nor every kind of
war, nor every way of conducting a war. And although it
sanctions war in principle, it does not sanction war in general. It
consents to war circumstantially—but not indiscriminately!

Principal elements of the Christian doctrine of just war are as
follows: (1) it must be just in its intent, namely, the restoration
of peace, justice, and order; (2) it must vindicate and establish
justice; (3) there must be a reasonable hope for victory; (4)
decision to engage in war must be made by and waged under the
proper authority—the ruler or rulers of the state; (5) the
conduct of war is to be just—there must be no excessive,

unnecessary violence and killing of civilians; (6) there should
be no engagement in war except as a last resort—after all means
have been exhausted to keep the peace; (7) destruction imposed upon the enemy is to be measured by the principle of
proportion—the evil of the war shall be no greater than the evil
to be corrected with a proper proportion between the degree of
guilt and the scope of punishment; and (8) war must be waged
in the spirit of compassion, reluctance, and repentance.

Protestant-Catholic Ethic

On December 23, 1956, Pope Pius XII made an historic
Christmas broadcast from Vatican City. He sanctioned the use
of force in defense against Communism. He recognized war as a
duty ("as a last resort") against Communist aggression.

The Pope recognized the apparent intentions of the enemy to
impose on all peoples, in one way or another, "a special intolerable way of life." He called for the unanimous and courageous
behavior "of all who lived the truth" to preserve peace and
freedom. He pointed out that it would be a fatal error to repeat
what happened during the years preceding World War II,
when threatened nations, and not merely the smallest, sought
their safety at the expense of others. In lamentation he recalled
that "in the end, all were together overwhelmed in the holocaust."

He emphasized that "a good course of action can never be
had by mere sentiment." He called for an objective appraisal of
such important questions as military service, weapons, and war.
He said, "It is clear that war—for effective self-defense and with
the hope of a favorable outcome against unjust attack—could
not be considered unlawful."

Protestant spokesman Eugene Carson Blake wants it to be
made clear that the great majority of Christians, including theo-
logians and ecclesiastical leaders, are not pacifists. While abhor-
ring war and believing that most wars are futile and that all are

sinful, one of the most widely held Christian positions is that force, even in its violent form, is not wrong in itself. The dominant Christian position is that force must be used with restraint and placed under the direction of righteousness. In pure candor, any contemplation of world order without some use of force, is considered idealistic and irrational. It is not therefore the Christian's duty to forego all use of force in a violent world like ours today.

Many people seriously question whether church leaders are competent to discuss political matters. There is further concern as to the competency of the clergy to dictate foreign policy or evaluate military involvements. The clergyman, of course, does not claim infallibility. He is the first to admit his limitation of judgment. He hopes only to make a contribution to the collective effort of the national quest for peace and the international settlement of war. (Many politicians do not hesitate to claim God's approval of their policies, so the minister feels that he may be excused for commenting on the political scene in the light of the Christian faith!)

The Christian minister knows that war never does really settle anything—but it may gain time and position for other and more spiritual forces to prevail.

Ministerial support of war and "constructive violence" has usually been identified with right wing elements—fundamentalist or conservative groups. It appears that there is an increasing objectivity in the liberal wing, however, possibly inspired by the role of the late German theologian, Dietrich Bonhoeffer, in a plot to kill Hitler in World War II.

One of the most powerful and influential critics of pacifism in our country has been Reinhold Niebuhr of New York City. A former professor of Christian ethics at Union Theological Seminary, Dr. Niebuhr has reflected a lifetime struggle with the ethical implications of participation in war. For many years he was prominently identified with the pacifist position. Then he broke away and developed a most devastating critique on the pacifistic ideology.

In his book *Christianity and Power Politics,* Niebuhr offers a rationale for Christian participation in war. He emphasizes that Christianity is not simply a philosophy of love; such only distorts and confuses the issue. He attempts to apply Christianity to the total dimension of human existence. He deals with both the dynamics of love and the irrefutable fact of sin.

Dr. Niebuhr believes that most modern forms of pacifism are heretical and sometimes insincere. He documents the claim that too frequently they are based purely upon the Renaissance emphasis of the essential goodness of man. He points out that the typical pacifist tends to reject the Christian view of original sin, espousing the idealistic assumption that perfect love guarantees victory over the world.

An Archbishop's Views

Roman Catholic Archbishop Robert E. Lucey believes that war is an instrument of peace. Wars are necessary because "there are evil men in the world." One of the twenty-two election observers sent to South Vietnam by President Johnson in 1967, the prelate defended war as a moral tool in the interest of liberty and justice. He supported his statements at a news conference with excerpts from wartime messages of Pope Pius XII and Vatican II Pastoral Constitution on "The Church and the Modern World."

"It is necessary to use force and the man who doesn't believe in force will soon be a slave," said the Archbishop. "You cannot have peace in the world without force because there are evil men in the world."

Archbishop Lucey contended that the "doves," advocating peace at any price, were prolonging the war. He believed that a unilateral withdrawal of our forces would be not only a tremendous cruelty but also "a tremendous stupidity."

A Christian Rationale

Succinctly, there appear to be three valid reasons for participation in war: (1) to maintain, to restore or to create a climate
of stability and an environment of order within which government, under law, can function effectively; (2) because we will
not accept the alternatives resulting from noninvolvement—the
very thoughts of which are repugnant to us; (3) if freedom is
denied or threatened in any part of the world, it is to some
extent a threat to us.

In response to queries from the disciples regarding the
death-struggle between good and evil, Jesus concedes and un-
derlines the inevitability of crisis in a world marked by revolt
against God and at enmity against itself. Hate and violence are
to be anticipated. Suffering, bloodshed, and death will continue
to be the lot of mankind. We will make every conceivable effort
to educate, convert, improve and redeem the social situation.
But realism dictates our anticipation of and our preparation for
occasional violence at the respective levels of human encounter.

History has presented many situations in which the alternatives were clear: to fight or to surrender! Appeasement has
sometimes served as a temporary measure to gain time to
prepare for more effective resistance, but it never causes an
aggressor to desist. On the contrary, it encourages him to further aggression and merely postpones the decision to fight or
surrender. The conflict is one of opposing wills, expressed in the
clash of military arms. Any destruction beyond that which is
believed necessary to accomplish the mind-change of the aggressor and bring about a settlement of the war issues is unjustifiable
and therefore, unethical. But the issues must be faced and faced
courageously.

This again brings up the question of preparedness. A nation
unprepared for war is like a city unprepared for a robbery!
Unpreparedness is a sin. At the beginning of World War II and

also at the outbreak of hostilities in Korea, our nation was unprepared. Our forces were inadequate and incompetent. For two long years, both in Europe and Asia, thousands of our men were killed simply because we were no match for the enemy!

There is evidence of much muddled thinking on this subject in our country. Should a man be condemned because he dares to defend his home, his wife, and his children? Shall a city be condemned because it maintains a police force, training them in gunnery and hand-to-hand combat as a deterrent to the sinister forces of evil which stalk the streets at night? Shall a nation be condemned and defamed (by its own citizens!) simply because it endeavors to save its freedoms and its religious heritage? Shall tyranny and aggression be permitted to dissipate and destroy these hard-won values?

Sincere and sensitive people ask, "Is it going to be necessary to maintain a standing army at such enormous cost?" The answer is, "Yes." It is going to be necessary until men learn that wars do not pay. It is going to be necessary until all the nations of the earth recognize and are convinced that in a world war everybody loses and nobody really gains anything. But when one nation is determined ruthlessly to oppress the other nations of the world, it will be necessary for freedom loving peoples to come to their defense.

The dream of a warless world is a worthy one—but it is still only a dream. It is unrealistic. It is irrational. World peace awaits world government, and world government can be established and sustained only by a responsible and adequate police force. It follows that the police force will be trained to use *real force*. Such will be exercised with real restraint. But as long as there is sin in the world, force and violence will be the only language some men will understand!

In an unrighteous world peace is not always the greatest good nor war the worst evil. Peace which promotes injustice is worse than war in the cause of justice. Christianity must always take the side of a just and durable peace and oppose an unjust war. By the same token the Christian conscience demands participation in a just war as opposed to the tolerance of an unjust peace.

It must be admitted that one of the most common inclinations is to rely too much upon force. We must not suppose that armies, arms, and armaments alone can make a nation safe. The majority of modern Christians believe that the only kind of power that does not set up at least an equal resistance to it is the power of love. But love, itself, must be discriminating and must be permitted to dictate the greater good.

Direction in a Dilemma

In the New Testament the officers of the state are seen as ministers of God just as much as pastors are ministers of the church. (Rom. 13:2; 1 Peter 2:13–14) They may vary in their sense of divine calling, but their responsibilities to God and humanity are similar. Both are servants of God according to their sphere of calling. Because of this, the officials are to be obeyed "for the Lord's sake." To break the laws of man or the state, is at the same time to break the laws of God!

We can rightfully conclude that it is a sin to fail to cooperate with the state, both in its laws and its leadership. Christians can have no part with anarchists! Their religion will not allow them to be disloyal citizens of their country.

There are those who insist on an exception to this rule: They say that a citizen may disobey his state (government) if and when the state orders him to "sin." They cite the situation which developed when Peter opposed the rulers of his country when they commanded that he and the other apostles stop preaching about Jesus. In response he vowed to "obey God rather than men."

It should be crystal clear to any thinking person that literally applied this makes every man the law unto himself. The inevitable result is anarchy. Our nation is in the grip of such threatened tyranny of lawlessness right now. The individual citizen, no matter how pious or intelligent he may be, should think a long time before he deliberately defies the law of his land or the authority of his elected leaders!

Most of us will neither refuse to serve in government roles nor commit ourselves as all out advocates of war. Assuming that we can agree that aggressive warfare is unjustifiable, then we must establish criteria for evaluating the factors in each single war. The fundamental issues in these respective conflicts become very confused. They are often difficult or impossible to delineate and properly evaluate. We can never know all the facts. In our time much basic information must remain "classified" in the very interest of national security. It seems improbable that any private citizen or group of citizens is justified in claiming complete knowledge of a given international situation.

Yet we have an inescapable responsibility to try. We cannot avoid involvement. It is our duty to think, discuss, and debate the issues and to seek a responsible understanding of what is involved. But the Christian can neither reflect nor endorse the insidious arrogance which ignores the facts and impugns the motives of our leaders.

The responsible Christian understands that his failure or refusal to share in such duties will only prolong the agony and incur further jeopardy of law and life. The "demonstrators" apparently do not realize this. By trying to interfere with the due process of culminating the conflict they only prolong it. The Vietnam war is a case in point. We have documented evidence that as soon as Hanoi learned of certain mass protest movements and ugly demonstrations her leaders took new hope that America would withdraw, cancel our objectives, and surrender our aims in Southeast Asia. Certain tactical adjustments were made at different times as a result of these observations and an unknown number of American lives was the price of this abuse of the right to protest!

Christians hate war. They understand fully that war is against the will of God. It is hell and death and destruction. They participate with reluctance. It is the lesser of two evils. But responsible Christians are convinced that it is the will of God for his people to lay down even life itself for the inherent dignities of freedom and human rights.

The peoples of America have wanted peace so badly that we have practically gone on our knees to every major leader of the world begging them to use their influence to bring peace. During the Vietnam conflict, within the space of only four months, our emissaries made thirty-two peace offers—every one turned down with scorn!

We begin to ask ourselves how we can live at peace with those who do not want peace except at the price of capitulation. Because of this, we fight on, although we do it with sad and broken hearts. We cannot rejoice over the news reports of the enemy killed or his cities bombed. We support the war because we must. There is nothing else for us to do if we are going to hold up the principles actually and literally inherent in our religious faith.

We face a deadly dilemma. If we listen to the anti-war demonstrators we will favor immediate unilateral withdrawal. But such action could mean the progressive death of freedom. On the other hand, to press for a quick settlement of the war could possibly mean not only "totalcide" but actual annihilation of our civilization.

In this valley of dilemma we stand. Our American leaders have demonstrated an amazing and becoming restraint. Nevertheless, they are resolute in their commitment. We will continue to ask God for his guidance; we will preach, pray, and discuss the issues as intelligently and responsibly as we can. In the meantime, we must do the right as God gives us grace to see the right.

The Will to Peace

God's ideal for this world, his world, is peace. For reasons only partially understandable by us frail humans, God did command ancient Israel to wage war. But war is never lifted as the ideal. It is always seen as a reluctant alternative. God's plan is for peace.

It is easy enough to document this claim. David was denied the realization of his temple dream because he had "shed much blood and waged great wars" (1 Chron. 22:8–9). Israel was encouraged always to "pray for the peace of Jerusalem" (Psalm 122:6). God's people were led to anticipate a day when "love and faithfulness will meet; righteousness and peace will kiss each other" (Psalm 85:10).

The eighth-century prophets clearly envisioned an era of peace on earth. Isaiah prophesied a golden age: "And they shall beat their swords into plowshares, and their spears into pruning hooks: nation shall not lift up sword against nation, neither shall they learn war any more" (Isa. 2:4, KJV). He hails the coming Messiah as the Prince of peace. Micah promises that the time will come when men shall learn war no more.

The New Testament ethic is more person-directed than nation-directed, and the peace motif becomes more and more dominant as the plan and purpose of God for the life of man.

Jesus Christ was born to the sound of angels proclaiming, "Glory to God in the highest, and on earth peace among men with whom he is pleased" (Luke 2:14). Christ, himself, underscored the theme when he said, "Blessed are the peacemakers, for they shall be called sons of God" (Matt. 5:9). In a moving message to his disciples, Jesus said, "Peace I leave with you, my peace I give unto you" (John 14:27, KJV).

Jesus revealed God as a father of unspeakable compassion and love. He emphasized the fact that these qualities are to be reflected in his followers—even to the point of loving their enemies. This kind of peace is characterized not only by the cessation of hostilities but particularly by the presence of an active goodwill—overcoming evil, hatred, and war.

The Christian Ideal

This ideal is clear enough. Christians are assured of grace and forgiveness when we fail to attain this holy objective, but it serves as a continuing magnet toward which we are attracted. When Jesus commanded his followers to "be perfect," he realized that man can never be perfect as God is perfect. He simply commanded the disciples of love to keep on dreaming, keep on growing, and keep on reaching toward that godly ideal!

The Christian, in a warped and sinful world, confronts the dilemma of conflicting values and changing situations. We are sometimes overwhelmed by the evidence of injustice and ill will in our world. But we have enough of the nature of God within us to cling to the ideal and respond in sympathy to all who are victimized by injustice, violence, and war. We begin to be conditioned to resist evil doers, not simply for selfprotection, but out of genuine interest in others—all others!

We know that peace is something more than appeasement. We must have warm hearts and clear heads. There are no neat schemes or handy blueprints. But the biblical ideal is our magnetic pole by which compasses are set, directions are determined, and constructive actions are inspired. God leads his people toward the lofty ideal.

Who Is for Peace?

Unfortunately the *will* to peace is less pronounced than the *desire* for peace. And the most sophisticated safeguards against war will be futile without the will of the people to achieve and maintain peace.

In listing the aphorisms by which the practical politicians seem to live, the late Alben Barkley used to lead off with the pronouncement that "everybody is for peace—some." The people, he believed, admire a fighter—but only if he is fighting back!

It is amazing how much universal application Barkley's Law seems to have attained. Everybody who makes war denies any lust for conquest. We can almost convince ourselves that Hilter's armies overran Europe because they felt they had to do so in defense of the Third Reich. Similarly, when the Red Guards were sent swarming against the presumed enemies of Mao's revolution, it is interpreted as "a protective impulse." Warmongers all seem to be able to convince themselves that their gestures are defensive—never offensive!

It may indeed be one of the modern ironies that the world's leaders are speaking the truth when they refer to their own peoples as peace-loving. Perhaps it means that it is largely a failure in communication that prompts lovers of peace to send their sons forth to do battle with the sons of foreigners who share their aversion to armed aggression!

It may be argued that the United Nations is both proof and product of this proposition. Even the tough-minded politicians who complain that the UN is all talk and no action concede that while men are talking they aren't usually fighting. (Of course their brothers may be slugging it out across the way!) If the members on some occasions seem to engage in a meaningless minuet, and others hurl epithets more abrasive than those employed on most waterfronts, they are tacitly expressing their constituents' view that such exchanges still are preferable to the mortal combat for which they may serve as substitute!

The very word peace is highly ambiguous. It means different things to different people. Somewhere the French aviator-writer, Saint Exupery, has described peace as the time when each man has a home to which to return at the close of the day. For the Communist, peace is that situation in which the tensions of the world revolution have finally been resolved, the state disappears, and the man lives in utopia. For those who have become committed to the ideals of freedom and personal liberty, peace means something more—much more!

Peace means far more than simply the absence of war. A peace which is genuine and lasting is always characterized by freedom, justice, truth, and love. Peace is really dynamic and creative in nature. It is more than a proclamation. It is more than the resolutions which we pass in our Christian bodies or governmental assemblies.

Words without intents and actions are meaningless. War cannot be destroyed by merely talking about peaceful dreams and objectives. Peace is more than programming. A crusade of activity promoting peace can actually be motivated by a warring spirit. Peace requires not only *doing* something but *being* something. The individual Christian is supposed to be the human embodiment of our Lord's picture of peace.

How Wars Begin

Little Willie looked up from his homework and said to his mother: "Mummy, how do wars begin?"

She replied: "Well, dear, World War I began because Germany overran Belgium."

But her husband, who had fought in that war, interrupted and said: "That wasn't the beginning of it."

His wife was annoyed and replied: "Willie didn't ask you. He asked me."

"Well," said her husband, equally exercised, "for goodness sake, tell him the facts and not fairy tales."

To which his wife replied: "Why do you want to interrupt? Nobody asked your opinion!"

Husband and wife continued to lash one another until at last Willie looked up again and said: "It's all right, Mummy. I think I know how wars begin."

We all know very well that war is not the nexus of human conflict. It is, rather, an extension of the little wars in our own hearts and homes. Think of the schemes and tensions which emerge from individuals and families. Reflect upon the hostilities apparent between a man and his wife, between parents and children, between children and children. Ponder the conflicts and jealousies, the tauntings and hatreds that develop in schools, offices, shops, and clubs. Add now the rivalries and competitions, the cliques that exclude and the bitter animosities that resent exclusion. Remember the divisions of races and cultures, economics—and even religion!

A deacon in a Baptist church vowed, "As long as I am a member of this church, ain't nothing ever goin' to be unanimous." There is more of this spirit than we would like to admit. Such destructive compulsions in people who claim to be Christian are easy to record and document.

Psychologists believe that war is a symptom of human unhappiness. They theorize that subconsciously men permit and aggravate the conditions of war in an effort to escape meaninglessness, boredom, frustration, and fear. It follows that a man who experiences no genuine satisfaction in life does not really care whether he lives or dies in such condition. And to accept "peace" as synonomous with his undesirable situation looms only as the sealing of his doom.

The question recurs: "How much do we want peace?" Do we desire peace enough to seriously evaluate the maze of modern life and do something to bring meaning where there is meaninglessness? Do we want it badly enough to turn our capacities for war into the quest for peace?

The Quest for Peace

In an address at the 1966 seminar on "Christianity and World Issues," Arthur H. Goldberg succinctly noted the role of war in the modern world: "Ours is a different world in that a total war is now excluded as a policy among men. Total peace is now our objective. We have been at least partially successful in that we do not have total wars; but the absence of total peace continues to challenge us."

On Monday, December 8, 1941, the day after Pearl Harbor, President Franklin D. Roosevelt spoke to the nation. Paralyzed by the sudden realization of our involvement in another World War, we listened with our hearts in our throats! The President reminded the nation that without doubt the industrial and manpower resources of the United States were adequate to win the war. Then he made it a point to say that this time, we must also win the peace! That task, he pointed out, would be largely assigned to the educators and the Christian church.

Today, in retrospect, we recognize that the battlefield soldier acquitted himself marvelously and accomplished his task—with the aid of a mighty industrial compact and the collaboration of the great scientists of the free world. We are haunted, however, by the realization that education and religion did not follow through as adequately as we intended. We are still struggling to achieve the peace.

Through the centuries, seers and prophets have worked out in considerable detail various proposals for the attainment of this illusive objective. Some of their plans have been purely visionary while others were quite realistic. Step-by-step these ideas have become more and more sophisticated and practicable.

As far back as the fourteenth century a plan for peace was worked out by Pierre Dubois, who advocated a federation of

Christian sovereign states, and was the first to suggest "an
international court of arbitration." Dante conceived of a worldwide state with power vested in a single ruler to suppress
tyrannies and bring about universal peace. Sixteenth-century
scholars and diplomats pondered "an assembly of ambassadors
representing various sovereigns" suggested by Emeric Cruce.
His plan was the first to recommend a worldwide organization
which embraced both Christian and non-Christian nations.
Henry IV is credited with significant concepts toward a balance
of power between the sovereign nations.

In 1625 Hugo Grotius published his "The Rights of War and
Peace" which is recognized as a truly classical work in its field.
The concept of international law was now firmly established in
the minds of world leaders. The eighteenth and nineteenth
centuries saw further development of a design of a world organization and a world court. Immanuel Kant's "Perpetual Peace"
represented a new level of attainment when published in 1795.

Since the Napoleonic Wars (1815) the use of international
conferences as a means of settling international disputes has
been steadily gaining ground. The Hague Conventions of 1899
and 1907 involved several nations in a Permanent Court of
Arbitration. These peace conferences appear to be the first truly
international assemblies meeting in time of peace for the purpose of preserving peace.

The League of Nations

To Woodrow Wilson must be credited the next significant
step in the movement toward world organization for peace. Out
of his creative mind and idealistic spirit came a concept which
was primarily a part of the peace settlement following World
War I. We cannot hold him responsible for its failure! But lack
of unity between the United States and her European allies—
and especially the tension between Great Britain and France—
severely handicapped its function.

The League of Nations was trapped by its own environment. Some said it was ahead of its time. At the risk of a historical oversimplication, we will simply conclude that there were not enough responsible men on the international scene to take advantage of this brilliant and promising pattern for peace!

In spite of its weaknesses, the League of Nations must be credited with many accomplishments, particularly in its early days. Then it ran into significant obstacles in the 1930's. Japan waged war against China (1931) and the League was ineffective in efforts to intervene. Its influence was further weakened by the terrible economic depression of the era. It was powerless in 1935 when Italy marched against Ethiopia and completely impotent in dealing with the German ravages of Europe in the late years of the decade. With the outbreak of World War II, it was functionally dead. It was declared so officially by a resolution passed at the last meeting of its assembly in April, 1946.

United Nations

The League of Nations died but the idea of world government persisted. The League's assembly became the General Assembly of the United Nations. The former's Council is the Security Council of the latter. The Permanent Court of International Justice was adopted by United Nations.

The Moscow Declaration of October 30, 1943, laid the groundwork for a new international organization. The United States, the United Kingdom, the Soviet Union, and China were the first formal participants. The Declaration included some of the purposes and principles stated in the Atlantic Charter which had been signed by the President of the United States and the Prime Minister of the United Kingdom on August 14, 1941.

The next major step in the preparation for the organization of the United Nations was the meeting, in the fall of 1944, of representatives of the great powers at Dumbarton Oaks, near Washington. From this meeting emerged the general outline for the organization of the United Nations. The Yalta Conference in February of 1945 established a voting procedure in the proposed Security Council.

The San Francisco Conference of April 25, 1945, was disappointing in many respects, but it did implement the activity which resulted in ratification of a new charter on October 24, 1945.

Participants and observers soon recognized that the big problem confronting the organization was the relationship between the two major powers of the world—the United States and the U. S. S. R. It was readily apparent that there could be no ultimate stability unless these two powers could learn to get along with each other. Here emerged the crux of coexistence.

The modern world situation is somewhat comparable to the conditions which developed in our cities with the arrival of the automobile. Before the advent of the motor car or when cars were the possession of the favored few, we got along very well, although there were some occasional collisions. There came a time, however, when it was necessary to set some very elaborate traffic rules. These rules seriously limit the individual's rights in the interest of the safety of the community.

So it is with the global community. With vastly improved communication and a greatly contracted world, freedom of movement becomes more touchy and dangerous. National interests are bound to clash, and such clashes are pregnant with peril. So we draft "traffic rules" for the world, and such rules inevitably limit the rights of some for the good of all!

In the United Nations we have a world organization which deliberately assumes this function. It must be an organization in which all nations will be bound together, not by force alone, but united in a dynamic dedication to a great common purpose and conviction—that peace can and must be established on this earth!

The UN has labored under unbelievable handicaps. It is not a super-state. It is not even a federal union of nation-states. It possesses no real sovereignty. It is simply a loose conglomeration of national bodies, some of whom sometimes appear to be committed to enmity against one another!

But a fair judgement would insist that the UN has performed impressively considering the adverse circumstances under which it has been forced to function. It does, after all, provide a forum for the expression of the world's collective moral conscience, and there is every reason to believe that this concentration of consciences has served many purposes which cannot readily meet the eye.

In addition to its political and military significance, the UN provides a channel of communication and negotiation for food distribution, population control, aid to children, literacy, scientific cooperation, and world trade.

The Vision Emerges

Nobody has claimed that the United Nations organization is a perfect instrument. Criticisms and dissatisfactions are numerous. Yet it is the only organization for peace the world now has. It may not be the answer and certainly is not the last word, but it has an important function to perform and our hope rests substantially in developing it—not abandoning it! In spite of its weaknesses, it deserves our confidence and our public support. The thinking Christian will recognize that in the world today the United Nations is his only channel for international implementation of the concept of peace.

The fact that peace is so hard to attain does not mean that its possibilities are negligible. Christian people should make certain that they hold high the hope for the implementation of the Master's ideal. Realism forces us to recognize that as long as there are people in the world who are not motivated by love and justice, emergency action involving the application of force may be required. We will continue to utilize this resource where absolutely necessary while waging the larger war, on a world-wide scale, for justice, equality, and fraternity.

Let none dare deter or intimidate us in pursuit of our "dream!" Dreams precede realities—and some dreams come true. Something like this must be what God intended and it is what good men desire. We should indulge ourselves in no rest until we achieve this end. Christians must keep the vision clear and walk in the way of personal peace ourselves. We must cultivate a passion for peace. We must dwell upon its beauties and worship at its shrine. If we lay our best in plans and skills as a sacrifice upon its altar, it will come and abide with us. It may come sooner than we think. Sentiment is stronger than armies.

Let us remember that witchcraft, a heritage of the ages, was completely stamped out in a single decade by a deliberate and significant change in human sentiment. With the death of Hamilton, duelling was given its death blow by the sudden precipitation of sentiment which had long been uneasy but inert.

So it is with this growing and widespread sentiment for world peace. The elements seem to be falling into place. We have the intelligence, and we can generate the compassion! We have the brains, and Christian zeal can be made to spread like wildfire in generating an adequate enthusiasm. We must have a will for peace!

What the Church Can Do

On the occasion of the Japanese surrender in 1945 General MacArthur declared: "The problem [of war] basically is theological, and involves a spiritual recrudescence and improvement of human character. It must be of the spirit if we are to save the flesh."

The task of the church is primarily in the realm of the spirit. Christ's commission binds us to this ministry to persons, to characters, and to dispositions. Our task is the proclamation and demonstration of the gospel of repentance and reconciliation.

We are to pray for peace and work for peace. We must build bridges of understanding between individuals, groups, and nations.

In the early church "peace" came to be understood as an internal quality. Spiritual men were to be men of peaceful disposition and intention. The word meant not only the absence of war, but also the absence of general bitterness and contention. Paul exhorts Christians to a life of gentleness and meekness in which patience and devotion are manifested toward one another in love.

Paul taught that it is only when men are at peace with God that they can be at peace with one another. If hostilities and strife between men are to be eliminated, peace will have to flow from man's relationship with God.

At best, civil government can only create an external framework in which men of good will can make peace a reality by injecting into its structures the genuine peace of God. Ultimately, there is only one thing that will inspire man to observe treaties and respect the mutual interest—irrespective of the cost —and that is spiritual regeneration!

The Prince of Peace

This is precisely what Jesus talked to Nicodemus about in the third chapter of John. It is precisely what Jesus envisioned as he marched up the long and painful *Via Doloroso*. It is a spiritual fundamental and a fact of logic that the inner man must be changed before the outer responses can be adequately controlled. At the heart of the world problem is the problem of the human heart. This is the one indispensable and inescapable mission of the church. It has been so through the centuries. It will not change.

This becomes the premise of the Christian ethic. Make the tree good and the fruit will be good. A corrupt tree cannot be expected to bring forth any other than corrupt fruit. Once the heart is yielded, deliberately and continuingly, to the mind and spirit of the Master, then teaching, training, and ethical guidance can be effective. Until then, it has little or no chance.

Paul taught that when a man becomes a Christian he is a "new creature" for "old things are passed away" and "all things are become new." In loyalty to this conviction, the saints have died and the martyrs have witnessed beyond the grave. They believed devoutly that man's hope lies in the supernatural transformation of his mind and heart by the redemptive love of God.

This accounts for the words of the apostle Paul who said: "And be not conformed to this world; but be ye transformed by the renewing of your mind, that ye may prove what is that good, and acceptable, and perfect, will of God" (Rom. 12:2, KJV).

Many will ask, "Why not adopt some other religion as the unifying factor for civilization? Why not try Buddha, or Confucius or a Zoroaster or Mohammed?" Some will suggest a syncretistic "mixing" of the best elements of all.

The Christian must answer that Jesus Christ is unique among all of the religious personalities of the centuries. We believe that he—and he alone—suffered, died and arose from the grave, even as he promised, in triumph over sin and death. He, and he alone, offers us a sure and certain basis for our faith and our only living hope. He, and he alone, makes all men brothers and he is our peace. "For he is our peace, who hath made both one, and hath broken down the middle wall of partition between us" (Eph. 2:14, KJV).

Someone has said that no possible arrangement of bad eggs will make a good omelet. It is equally true that no possible arrangement of men and maps, as they are, will result in peace. There is something in the spirit of man which makes for misunderstanding, bloodshed, and destruction. It is within the spirit of man that we must find the answer to the problem of war. We must redeem the spirit if we are going to save the flesh!

Peace begins with persons. It has always been that way. It

becomes national only as it becomes a climate of reality among persons. How can there really be peace between nations until there is peace within the respective states? How can there be peace in the states before there is peace in the cities? How can there be peace in a city until there is peace in her communities, schools, churches, and homes? How can there be peace in these social units until there is peace in the individual hearts of the constituents? And how can there be peace in any human life until that life has been dynamically related to the source of peace?

Blessed Are the Peacemakers

No wonder peacemakers are called the sons of God! To speak of a Christian who is not a peacemaker by commitment is to use a contradiction in terms. Peacemaking is a vocation shared by all followers of the Prince of peace. The Christian will rejoice in every opportunity to create good will and build better understanding among men. This begins in the heart and character of the individual. It reflects itself first in the family. It overflows into the community, the church and the town.

Booker T. Washington, reflecting the spirit of his Lord, declared, "I will not let any man reduce my soul to hatred." It was said of Henry Ward Beecher that no one ever felt the full force of Beecher's kindness until he had done Beecher an injury! Such attitudes and commitments make for peace among men. Positively and actively—not just passively—each Christian must make his contribution toward such a social atmosphere. Collectively, deliberate efforts will join Christians as creators of such a climate.

George Lansbury was one of England's tireless workers for peace. He spent all of his mature life wrestling with the knotty problems which are related to war. He lived through World War I and died at the outbreak of World War II. Often discouraged, but never doubting the efficacy of his labors, he literally gave himself to the cause of peace. Some of his friends, however, did not understand. One of them asked him one day how much nearer he thought peace was as a result of his efforts. Lansbury replied, "Forty years nearer!"

One wonders how many of us are really qualified to be "peacemakers" as Christ seems to have implied. It is not simply a matter of knowing the right words. It is more than the mouthing of a few pat panaceas. Christ was talking about the cast of a man's character. He had in mind the dynamics of spiritual disciplines. It is a matter of commitment, maturity, and mission.

1. In order to be a Christian peacemaker one must have first of all found his peace with God! The God of the Bible must have become the basic fact and factor in his life and witness. The God of our Lord Jesus Christ must have become the touchstone of all meaning and destiny. Christ, himself, must have become the integrating center of his otherwise fractured and shattered being.

2. The Christian peacemaker must be one who has found peace with himself. His identification with God has made life sensible and meaningful. He becomes involved. Words are not enough; he becomes absorbed in acts and deeds. This dynamic, outgoing quality of life becomes wholesome and creative. It is going somewhere. It is treading the highroad of noble purpose and fine ideals. It grows, becoming progressively richer and stronger. The strands of personality become united in a holy task. He is at peace with himself!

3. The Christian peacemaker must have achieved that state of maturity which not only enables him but conditions him to live in personal peace with others. He will take the initiative in peaceful attitudes and actions. When rebuffed or rejected, the Christian peacemaker will not walk away in anger, calling down fire and brimstone upon his adversary. He will bear his witness to the reality of the love of God in human relations. He will

control his tongue, his actions, and his own plans. He will "seek peace and pursue it."

4. The Christian peacemaker must possess the equipment to be an instrument in peacemaking between others. By the time a person has found peace with God, with himself, and with others, he will certainly have acquired certain characteristics which are essential to this fourth level of peacemaking. He will be trusted by others because he is trustworthy. He will not be feared because he has established a posture of love and peace—instead of hatred and war.

Signs of Hope

Today it is evident that there is a resurgence of the peace movement in the world. Renewed optimism is evident in the United Nations. Practically every constituent body has gone out of its way to present itself as a peace-loving society. There are some new factors in our time which make peace a probability —at least the avoidance of war.

First is the awful and terrible threat of nuclear escalation. This is a definite deterrent to irresponsible and inflammatory gestures.

Second, we are at a point in history where it may be technically possible to provide the minimum essentials of life for all people, and thus alleviate some of the most serious historical motivations toward war.

Third, we rejoice in the rapidly increasing number of fields of international cooperation. Many nations are working closely together in development of the sciences, dealing with the problems of food, medicine, over-population, and conservation of resources. Impressive and significant exchanges are being made in the fields of the humanities and religion.

Fourth, we are seeing a great advance in the means of worldwide communication. For the first time in history a well-informed worldwide public opinion may be had, assessed, and projected. Peace-loving people see great promise in these new techniques.

Fifth, world trade is finally coming into its own. We are nearing the day when all people may have the opportunity to produce or buy the things they need and to sell the things they produce. The inherent values of such two-way progress goes far beyond the economic. It can have great psychological and political effect upon international relations.

Sixth, we now have on a limited but significant scale a legal framework for the whole world. Limited and inadequate as they are, these structures represent the beginnings of a body of international law.

All these things conspire to remind us that we are living in an altogether different kind of world from that which men have ever known before! It is a world in which it is now actually possible to do something about the persistent problem of war. We will, of course, avoid looking for neat, easy, overnight solutions. Progress has come painfully and continued progress means continued pain. But the dream is worth the effort.

We emphasize again that it is foolish to consider simply laying down our arms in the face of continuing hostility. Neither can we expect hostility suddenly to vanish from the earth nor likewise the fears to which it gives rise. However, alert to danger, and accepting the responsibilities which defense and danger imply, we shall try to bridge the gulf. If we fail, then the church will have betrayed her Lord.

While the primary aim of the Bible is not international peace but individual redemption, the implications of salvation certainly reach out to embrace peace among men, not only in heaven but also on earth. Peace does not wait on God but upon God's people.

8

Alternative to Annihilation

History records a progressive degradation of warfare since the eighteenth century. In spite of the increased humanitarian sensitivity in Western civilization, many social practices have drifted in the opposite direction.

On the American frontier the code and character of the savages were appropriated by the civilized. New and vicious patterns emerged in man's inhumanity to man.

The Civil War gave rise to Sherman's "scorched earth" technique. With the technological revolution new weapons led to bloodier battles. Poison gas was invented. The airplane and bomb followed. They were both first used only to strike at troops and military installations.

In World War II bombing attacks came to be used to fracture the morale and break the resistance of civilian populations. This was called strategic bombing. Suddenly, Hitler began to employ "obliteration bombing" and the world was shocked. Churchill castigated this "new and odious form of attack." Within months, however, his own country had decided that it was necessary to retaliate in kind.

Then came the atom bomb—and the obliteration of Hiroshima and Nagasaki. Suddenly we are frightened, and we should be. We are in search for an alternative to annihilation!

The cynical Bertrand Russell has written frequently of the folly of war. The following (from *The Listener*, 12, 30, 54) is

111

typical: "Is our race so destitute of wisdom, so incapable of impartial love, so blind even to the simplest dictates of self-preservation, that the last proof of its silly cleverness is to be the extermination of all life on our planet?"

Two Dates in History

There are two dates of outstanding importance in the history of mankind. One is the turning point of all history, the date from which we reckon our calendars, the birth of Jesus Christ. At that moment, a person entered into the world with such force of example and persuasion that the entire lot of man was radically altered. He has become the most potent force for the healing and reconciliation of the world community which mankind has ever seen.

The other date is August 6, 1945—on which the first atomic bomb was dropped, and the city of Hiroshima was immortalized. In that moment forces were unleashed which may mean the end of human existence, and which in any case present a terrible antithesis to the spirit and purpose of the first event.

The terror and tension have become so great that somebody has wished for "the good old days when all we had to fear was fear itself."

Hiroshima and Nagasaki

At about seven o'clock on that fateful Sunday morning, the Japanese radar system reported the approach of a small force of enemy planes. Hiroshima and the surrounding towns were alerted. By eight o'clock it was determined that only three planes were in the formation. The alert was withdrawn on the assumption that the planes were on a routine or exploratory photographic-reconnaissance mission.

Shortly after eight-fifteen the National Broadcasting Company of Japan noticed that the Hiroshima radio was off the air. Attempts were made to reach the station by telephone. There was no response. At eight-thirty the radio officials were so worried that they asked the railroad telegraph station in Tokyo to try to reach Hiroshima. They were informed that the telegraph lines had been cut.

Then it was that the dramatic and frightening report began to emerge: A large explosion at Hiroshima had been seen by people thirty miles away!

Radio officials, still perplexed about this report, decided to notify the central government. The government in turn tried to reach Hiroshima by radio and through all conceivable military channels, but still no answer came.

The alarmed government officials took counsel of their fears. They knew that the various communication centers in Hiroshima were miles apart, and that there was no ammunition dump in the city. They were at a complete loss to understand what kind of explosion could have occurred to destroy all lines of communication. They reasoned that the three enemy planes which had been reported in the vicinity could not possibly have achieved such "obliteration."

Then the Japanese army sent a colonel to Hiroshima by plane to investigate the situation. What he saw while still a hundred miles from the city was obviously too much to comprehend. He had no background for such an experience. A huge pillar of smoke stretched unbelievably high into the air.

It was mid-morning by the time he reached the outskirts of the city and visual contact. He looked down in utter amazement at the mad scramble of people and the utter devastation of the city. He finally set his plane down at an airfield thirty miles away and began to talk to refugees who were streaming past. They told him that a large bomb had been dropped on their city, that terrible fires were raging through most of its streets, and that thousands must have surely perished.

The stunning story was quickly sent around the world: One of the three American planes had dropped the first atom bomb ever to be dropped on a city! The bomb had exploded with the power of twenty thousand tons of TNT. It was a blast equal to that of all the high explosive which could be carried in a fleet of two thousand heavy bombers.

The Bomb's Effects

The bomb fell near the geographical center of the city of 343,000 inhabitants and completely destroyed sixty percent of the city. The city's center was completely pulverized.

Twenty-six of the thirty-three fire companies were completely destroyed, and two-thirds of their eight hundred firemen killed. 260 of the city's 300 physicians and surgeons were killed and 1,800 of their 2,400 nurses.

Immediate deaths numbered around 100,000 and another 100,000 were injured—many of them much more seriously than was first thought because of the strange effects of the radiation. Many of those who lived—and even some who thought they were unscathed—have been reduced to a limited kind of existence because of the deformities and malfunctions.

The bomb which fell on Nagasaki a few days later was described as a different type. Its results, however, were much the same—a tremendous flash, a billowing mushroom of smoke, followed by death, destruction, suffering, and pain.

This event marked a distinct breakthrough in scientific achievement and made possible the extinction of entire cities and nations. The atom bomb, along with its successor, the hydrogen bomb, became recognized as so unbelievably destructive that they ushered in an entirely new era of warfare.

Several years ago a Methodist minister in Hiroshima and the pilot of the plane from which the bomb was dropped were brought together on a live television program. When asked about their first thoughts at the time of the explosion, the minister said that he fell to the ground and said to himself, "Oh, God, what has happened?" The pilot said that when he circled the city and looked back at the tremendous mushrooms of smoke and fire, he cried out, "Oh, God, what have we done?"

We are still pondering the implications, and the more we understand about the event the more convinced we are that we have opened a Pandora's box of such unimaginable proportions that we shrink in horror from further contemplation.

Evangelists of Anxiety

Two groups of people were immediately articulate: Church-men were deeply troubled about the moral implications, and scientists began immediately to see a specter of a Frankenstein which would devour its own creators!

We slowly realized that we had won a Pyrrhic victory: We won the war, but at the terrible cost of an unbearable sense of moral guilt!

As exhilaration over ending the war subsided, this sense of guilt began to build up. Fear and shame balanced against a tentative and suspicious hope—these became the framework of our cautious probing and future designs.

Professor Harold Urey spoke for the scientists in his famous pamphlet, "I am a frightened man." The first line was, "I write this to frighten you," and his colleagues echoed his hysteria. They became the "evangelists of anxiety." Their appeal was measured and plaintive. They deplored the complacency of those who were unmoved and called it insanity!

On sober reflection it is not altogether unexpected that sudden possession of such great new power should have had such a shocking and perplexing effect. There is indeed a paradox implicit in the holding of such power: It excites both satisfaction and dread; we want it and yet we fear it! We behold this incredible power, and stand in awe: we do not know whether to laugh or cry. Slowly we begin to suspect that we have arrived at the profoundest level of the human spirit—its glory and its shame.

When Otto Hahn, the German scientist who had first split the atom in 1958, heard the news about Hiroshima, his impression was so profound that friends sat by him constantly for days lest he take his own life. A new age had been born, and no man understood it!

Nuclear Fallout

We are still studying the effects on those two Japanese cities, and the end is not yet in sight. Water sources have been contaminated and may not be cleansed for fifty years. Vegetation has been impregnated with death and will continue to be capable of destroying bone marrow throughout at least a generation.

Genes in the sex cells of uncounted thousands of persons have been thrown into confusion and may produce mutations a hundred years from now—some scientists say even longer. Incalculable radioactive destruction has been loosed in such a fashion that literally millions of people have been exposed to dangerous effects, tens of thousands of whom have not yet been born!

We are just beginning to grasp the fact that the detonation of certain nuclear weapons produces effects which have never existed anywhere in nature previous to the time of the explosions. Strontium 90, for example, may be the "most toxic substance known to man." Cesium 137 and Carbon 14 pose different but similarly unimaginable hazards to the health and survival of the race.

Strontium 90 invades the blood stream and produces bone cancer and leukemia. Cesium 137 attacks muscle tissue and emits gamma rays which injure the genes in the sex cells—the evil results of which will appear in future generations.

These two highly toxic substances are capable of altering the characteristics passed on in germ plasm. It has been established that they are capable of producing stillbirths and malformations of various kinds. They also heighten the susceptibility of a child to disease and are presently suspected as the basic cause of multiplied cases of general debility.

There are actually two different types of fallout, each of which wreaks its own havoc.

By far the more insidious and dangerous aspect of radioactive fallout comes weeks, months or even years after the explosion. The effects upon the human body are negligible until the particles are ingested with food, drink, or inhalation. They then become fixed in the bones or muscles and remain there, giving off destructive and disastrous rays for many years. A bone cancer victim may not be aware of any abnormal condition for many years after exposure or contamination. Moreover, the winds of the stratosphere can carry the radioactive particles to another continent where unsuspecting people would become infected.

Unfortunately, there is no known way by which mankind can immunize thimself against these radioactive fallout particles. This is the reason that nuclear fission cannot be employed even on a limited basis. It is nothing to play around with!

The Nuclear Standoff

The horrendous factor in international relations today is the nuclear bomb. The two super powers, the United States and the USSR, each have enough nuclear warheads to destroy most of the world's population. Several of the nations are making great strides in their own nuclear programs.

The nuclear factor has introduced remarkable restraint in the diplomatic communications between the United States and the USSR. We can only imagine what effect this factor must have had in settling the crises in Berlin and Cuba and in the handling of the Vietnam situation. It seems to act as a deterrent to careless words or precipitous actions, and it appears to have effected a shift in the focus of violence.

Going back through the nineteenth century and into the latter part of the eighteenth, most of the wars started between developed countries of Europe. Almost four hundred separate instances of armed conflict have happened since the end of World War II, and they took place almost entirely in the undeveloped countries.

We can be thankful that none of these wars resorted to nuclear tactics. Nevertheless, every such engagement is fought in the context of the nuclear standoff between the Soviet Union and the United States.

Men have always considered it prudent to "count the cost" before waging war. One of our Lord's parables revives this point of reference. Responsible leaders through the centuries have projected their situations into approximated comparisons between the cost and the conceivable gains. We have now come upon a time when each war must be seen as a potential collective suicide.

This nagging threat is considered by many to be the greatest spiritual problem of our times. Such a catastrophe would officially be a war between nations. Essentially it would be a war against God! After all, it is the work of God and not of man alone that has been placed in jeopardy. God's creative design, not only for the universe in general but the life of man in particular, is threatened.

It is frightening to consider the world situation without the UN! The constantly increasing quantity, destructiveness, and distribution of nuclear weapons makes the prospect frightening enough with all of the communication and negotiation which we can possibly muster! Without some such tribunal the prospect is a nuclear Armageddon—the nearest thing to the production of hell on earth the mind of man can imagine.

We must be alert to extreme right-wing pressures to push the panic button and do or say anything precipitously. This is a time for patience. The cold war atmosphere is an atmosphere of continuing negotiation. All reasonable options must remain open.

What Church Groups Can Do

Excerpts from the annual reports of the Social Service Commission of the Southern Baptist Convention demonstrate one of the constructive functions of such groups. The 1952 statement makes a typical appeal to its constituents:

1. Redouble our efforts to reconcile man with God.
2. Do not tolerate any complacency about war.
3. Combat a mood of hysteria or blind hatred.
4. Reject fatalism about war.
5. Oppose primary reliance on military strategy to meet Communist aggression.
6. Press for positive programs which have immediate possibilities for peace and justice.

As far back as 1895, this body was expressing its conscience: "Resolved . . . that we join the other conventions of Christendom in petitioning the governments of the world to resort to arbitration instead of war in settlement of all disputes that may hereafter arise among nations; and that for the purpose of effectually securing such arbitration, we favor the establishment of an International Arbitration Court or High Court of Nations."

In 1921 we said, "Resolved . . . we are glad to join other bodies in an endorsement of this seemingly, practical movement toward disarmament with the hope and prayer that our torn and bleeding world may be restored to peace under the guidance and benediction of the Prince of peace."

On May 9, 1963, we adopted the following: "It is the duty of Christians everywhere to seek peace with all men on principles of righteousness. In accordance with the spirit and teachings of Christ they should do all in their power to put an end to war."

In all candor, however, it must be admitted that the Christian church in nineteen centuries has made very little impact on the cause for international peace. Men continue to ignore righteous injunctions.

Partly because of the church's failure to achieve visible results in decreasing or eliminating war, human society has tended to try other methods. Each has proved and will continue to be unsuccessful on its own. The church must be aggressive in every facet of its ministry—none more urgent than the elimination of war and the cessation of human hostilities.

A man answered the doorbell one pleasant spring evening and received a visitor from a neighboring church. Thirty minutes later he was reporting to his wife about his experience. The visitor had invited him to his church and had talked with him earnestly about becoming a Christian. His wife remarked tartly, "It looks as though he could have tended to his own business!"

Her husband answered soberly, "Dear, if you could have been there and heard him as he talked with me, you would have gotten the impression that it was his business."

Sometimes the church's strategy must be the unilateral demonstration of compassion and goodwill. Both are hard to resist. Love is the golden key to the human heart.

A small boy put it in practical expression. "Ronnie treated me mean when we were playing ball. He made me mad. I went home and got my new baseball bat. I came back and found him. I let him use my new bat. Now Ronnie and I are friends." That is indeed the world's oldest peace plan.

Christian goodwill is something more than a pious and doubtful hope that a dog will not bite. It is a positive confidence and affection. Its contagion is the great miracle worker. It sooths aggressions and dissolves conflicts.

Involvement

It is absolutely imperative that Christian people and organized Christian groups shall be an active ally of democratic government. Democracy is indeed a bold adventure of spiritual idealism into the realm of political pragmatism. It can be successful only in those situations where dedicated and responsible people support it and adhere to it.

It is not enough for a congregation to be instructed in sound doctrine. One of the very first duties of the church is to thrust itself into the life of the nation and the community. At times it will be almost literally a visible and verbal conscience of the community. It will reflect social sensitivity and will inspire impeachable integrity. Anytime the church retreats from the world and takes refuge in its theological cloisters it will deserve the terrible fate that is certain to descend upon it. But when the church moves out to supply the motives, the inspiration, the inner power, and the convictions to fortify men's souls, it will have earned its own immortality.

Christians must become involved with the masses of mankind in such a way as to bring about strong influences for reconciliation and constructive goodwill. We can help correct some of the conditions which cause war—poverty, over population, insecurity, and fear. Anything that we can do to help alleviate suffering, ignorance, and unrest is a step in preventing further international suicide. The church is called into the world to help in the formation of attitudes, to cultivate aspirations, and provide motivation—toward the godly ideal!

Individual Responsibility

A young minister entered the bedroom of his six-year-old son to get a globe of the world for study. The little boy, not yet asleep, startled the father by asking, "Daddy, what are you going to do with my world?"

It is easy for us to assume that one individual cannot make any significant difference in the present world situation. We can even indulge the suspicion that one group or one church can do little or nothing of real significance. But this is not true. Great doors still swing on little hinges. Kingdoms still depend on the proverbial horseshoe nail. A small boy can still plug the leak in a dyke.

In my early ministry I became convinced that the cardinal sin of both ministers and laymen in the Southern Baptist Convention was the sin of pride. At first, my exposure to this protracted self-adulation was inspiring. I began to feel that I was the steward of an unspeakable trust—participation in the greatest and most God-blessed fellowship on earth! We were said to be "the greatest" of this, and "the greatest" of that—until it began to grate on my ears and conscience!

Then a strange thing happened. I began to suspect that this was not our greatest sin after all. My experiences in the pastorate, my observations of our denominational failures, and my humiliating exposure to the entrenched evils of our social situation gave me a different clue.

I concluded that we are probably the world's greatest practitioners of evasion and cowardice! We have known to do much more than we have been willing to do. A false humility has shrouded our failures. "I don't really count," "They won't miss me," "My opinion is not important," are typical of our escape techniques.

This is our greatest sin. We are privileged and powerful. We are redeemed and responsible. There is much that we can do and that we must do. I close with a few specific suggestions as a personal contribution to the alternative to annihilation.

A Personal Program

1. We can indulge in a healthy revival of national pride and loyalty. I am not talking about a "my country, right or wrong" attitude. We need to recover a wholesome sense of appreciation and regard for the heritage of freedom, justice, and dignity to which our nation was originally committed and for which she

still offers an opportunity unique on the face of the earth!

2. We can reexamine, reaffirm and renew our own personal Christian experience. Unless we maintain a vital and living fellowship with Jesus Christ it is unlikely that we will be able to sustain a healthy and constructive relationship to men.

3. We can make a conscientious effort to keep growing in our understanding of Christian discipleship, American citizenship, and world service.

4. We must develop a personal program for keeping alert, knowledgeable and responsible concerning the political, economic, and religious needs in the world.

5. We must commit ourselves to a truth-and-information way of life. The apostles of hate, discord, slander, and despair are at work night and day. The cold war has bred its share of immoral propaganda and outright falsehood. But truth is available. We must seek it, pursue it, and ferret it out of the malaise.

6. We can determine that, whatever our vocation or profession, our chief business as children of God is to share in a redemptive identity with Jesus Christ by means of our works and witness.

7. We must set ourselves to the revitalization of institutional Christianity. The church has not been abandoned by God—it has simply been misunderstood and misused by God's people!

8. We must strive daily to share and reflect a healthy relationship between things spiritual and material—not despising the latter but simply subordinating it as an instrument (an indispensable instrument!) of the life of man and the purpose of God.

9. We must strive daily to open our hearts and every area of our lives to the leadership of the spirit of God, seeking his will and developing an increasingly dynamic relationship with the living Lord.

10. We must remind ourselves that the commission which Jesus Christ gave to his disciples has never been withdrawn nor

has it been completely fulfilled! The exciting adventure of worldwide witnessing is still ours to share.

11. We must learn to be broad in our visions, wise in our decisions, and generous in our sympathies. We must teach the rising generation to carry the world in their hearts! (Some of them are beginning to teach us!)

12. We can recognize and encourage the commitment of the younger generation to unselfish service and higher ideals which they appear to espouse. We can help them to hold on to those ideals and translate them into constructive action strategies. We can challenge them to embrace and demonstrate the commitment of Edward Everett Hale:

> "I am but one
> But I am one.
> I can not do everything
> But I can do something.
> What I can do, I ought to do
> And by the grace of God, I will do!"

13. And we must give ourselves to prayer! We must pray for peace. Such praying will both follow and inspire involvement in depth. Such praying will identify us sympathetically with those who carry the unspeakably heavy burdens of state in our behalf.

We must learn to pray for our President—whether we like him or not, whether he is a member of our party or not, and whether he is running the country like we think he should! With the admission that he just might have keener insight than we have, more resources for assessing the total situation, and more adequate judgment for final decision—he deserves our prayers.

We can never hope to have peace in our country, much less in the world, until we learn to believe the best instead of the worst about our elected leaders. We shall elect the best men we

have, support them with our efforts and prayers—or replace
them through the provisions of our constitutional options. It is
awfully hard to pray for a man that we are criticizing, and
awfully hard to criticize a man for whom we are praying.

We can and we must link ourselves vitally and dynamically
with other Christian people for the communal blessing to our
own lives and the additional strength of group influence and
actions in the social situation. This will help remind us that
although we have respective individual responsibilities, there are
some things which we can do together which we cannot begin to
do separately. This is one of the reasons why Christ established
the church and made it his expressed intention that everyone of
his children participate in his life and ministry.

Alternative to Annihilation

From time to time the dream of a warless world has suffered
disappointment and disillusionment. The twentieth century
dawned with hopes running high. Scientists had declared that
"inevitable progress" would finally eliminate war, along with
many other undesirable elements in the life of man.

Karl Marx built a similar concept upon Hegel's dialectic
formula—thesis, antithesis, and synthesis. He envisioned a
world in this triangular process as if it were a chambered
nautilus climbing in a spiral ascent from one spacious room to
another until at last it would reach "the dome more vast."

It really appeared for a time that the long-awaited dream was
about to come true. John R. Mott capped it with his optimistic
program for the evangelization of the world in his generation!

But the first fifty years of this century blasted these hopes
again! Within that period we fought two world wars—the worst
in all history—and have appeared ever since the second to be
standing on the brink of a third. Is our hope of peace pure
fantasy? Is it an ill-founded dream—the irrational makebelieve
of a frustrated child?

H. L. Mencken, the brilliant writer and critic, once said: "I am convinced that another war is not only likely but inevitable, and so it seems to me to be hopeless to talk about peace." Sir Austin Chamberlain took a similar stand: "I have no formula for peace, and must confess that I distrust the judgment of those who say they possess one." Sigmund Freud, Dean Inge, Havelock Ellis, Henry Morgenthau and dozens of renowned contemporaries are of very much the same opinion.

Many Americans continue to affirm that war is inevitable, that peace is only a breathing spell. One senses an attitude of utter futility by which men are tempted to accept war as a fatal disease which baffles all techniques of treatment. But the dream will not die—the followers of the Prince of peace will not let it die!

So the dream persists. It is a Christian ideal which reflects perennial Christian hope and vitality. It began with those heralds who bore the glad tidings of Christ's coming into the world with the song of peace on earth and good will among men. The notes of that song fell upon ears familiar with the clash of arms and the march of enemies in battle. Its notes settled healingly over the hills and valleys of a little patch of land which had been the battleground of nations for centuries. Men and women took up the song and their children have passed it on from generation to generation. It will not now die.

In the Metropolitan Museum of Art in New York, Father Time may be seen beating a sword into a plowshare, with a lion at his feet and a lamb sleeping peacefully nearby. The dream of Isaiah lives on in bronze—but even more in the hearts of the disciples of him whom Isaiah invisioned.

We quickly concede the improbability of "perfect peace" in a world of imperfect men. What we invision is a "relative peace" among nations which enables the world to seek creative and constructive solutions to its difficulties and problems.

We know better than to anticipate the elimination of every

source of friction and disagreement, every conflict of interest and power. But we can seek—and we must seek—legitimate and non-destructive avenues by which these disagreements may be minimized and their related conflicts constructively adjusted.

Realism reminds us that a world without force, violence or sin is not a real possibility. But a world without armed and irresponsible warfare is a live option and a worthy goal!

DATE DUE

GAYLORD			PRINTED IN U.S.A.